# PEACHBLOW GLASS

## Collector's Identification & Price Guide

### Sean and Johanna S. Billings

Published by

**krause publications**

700 East State Street • Iola, WI 54990-0001

Please call or write us for our free catalog of antiques and collectibles publications. To place an order or receive our free catalog, call 800-258-0929. For editorial comment and further information, use our regular business telephone at (715) 445-2214.

Library of Congress Catalog Number: 00-107844
ISBN: 0-87341-971-5
Printed in the United States of America

# ❦ *Dedication* ❦

For Kayleigh,
In hopes that this book will further encourage
her interest in history

and

For all glass lovers,
In hopes that they may finally be able to properly
identify peachblow

# ❦ TABLE OF CONTENTS ❦

# Acknowledgments

This book would not have become a reality without the help of our friend and mentor, Louis O. St. Aubin, Jr. of Brookside Antiques. Because we don't collect peachblow, we needed the guidance of someone intimately familiar with it; that person was Louis. He spent many hours aiding our research and answering questions. Plus, he let us raid Brookside's photo files, where we were lucky to find many wonderful pieces, expertly photographed by Bill Pitt. He reviewed the manuscript, many of our photo captions and helped us with pricing. This book is a credit to his efforts as much as ours.

We must also thank Clarence Maier of the Burmese Cruet and Steve Hetherington of Glasstiques for contributing additional photos, and in the case of Clarence, especially valuable information on and photos of Wheeling peachblow reproductions.

Special thanks to Holly McCluskey of Oglebay Institute and Cynthia Pratt of the Walters Art Gallery for aiding us in getting photos of rare or unusual vases. Cynthia was especially accommodating to our last-minute requests!

Of course, our research would not have been possible without the aid of these same people and the libraries available at the museums. In addition to those mentioned above, we owe special thanks to the Rakow Library at the Corning Museum of Glass, whose staff was very helpful. Gay Taylor at the Museum of American Glass at Wheaton Village and her assistants were also helpful in our research as was a young woman at the library at the Huntingdon Museum of Art. Thanks also to Elizabeth at the patent depository at the Free Library of Philadelphia for her help, and to the West Virginia Museum of American Glass for L.G. Wright catalog pages.

Doing original research was especially exciting, and in this case it was possible by Harold and Judy Bennett who graciously invited us into their home, answered our questions, and allowed us to go crazy photographing their glass. Frank M. Fenton of the Fenton Art Glass Co. also made time to answer questions and helped us dig around in the factory storage room for examples of Fenton peachblow. He allowed us to photograph those plus various items from the factory museum. Most importantly, Frank graciously loaned us original catalog pages not only from Fenton, but Hobbs, Kanawha and A.A. Importing. Frank has been described by many in the glass world as a jewel for researchers, and that he is.

Frank arranged for Antique Publications to loan us the negatives of his original Hobbs catalog, so the fragile document would not have to go through the rigors of being photographed again. So Antique Publications also deserves a thank you. So does A.A. Importing, for kindly giving us permission to reprint a couple pages from their catalogs. Thanks also to Arnold Russell at Pilgrim Glass for providing us with color copies of their catalog pages showing peachblow.

The members of the National Imperial Glass Collectors Society, particularly Cliff McCaslin, Joan Cimini and Paul M. Douglas, were especially helpful, supplying information and other materials such as ads, catalog pages and even tags. We all appreciate the help of former Imperial employee Lucile Kennedy, who has helped many a collector of Imperial with her inside knowledge. Thanks also to fellow authors Gary Baldwin and Robert and Deborah Truitt for answering our questions concerning the possibility of Bohemian peachblow.

Many others aided this endeavor by contributing photos or allowing us to photograph a few items. Angie Hudock and Darlene Severn were especially patient, eagerly offering to retake photos when the first batch came out too dark. Fred Wishnie of Wishful Things did the same. Brian Severn was especially trusting, sending us a Webb peachblow punch cup to photograph, plus several pieces of Harrach for photographing and comparison. And of course, our friend Stu Horn sent us a few photos, plus invited us over to photograph some pieces on our own. He and his wife Sally always fed us too!

Although not every photo submitted made it into the book, we would like to thank everyone who sent a photo including: Grandma Patty's Antiques, Williamstown Antique Mall, GlimmerGlass Antiques, Sara Sampson Antiques, Bob and Marjorie McCleskey, Debbie and Cliff Lacy, Irmgard Schmidt, Melissa M. Kleinfeld, Kay Knott, Ruth Sparks, Louise Nadeau and Barbara Loudon. We chose also to acknowledge each contributor in the photo captions. If the person took the photo, it will say "photo courtesy of ...." If we took the photo, it will say "Collection of ..." or "Courtesy of ..." The only exception is with the Severns, who wanted all of their items to be identified as "The Severn Collection," whether they took the photo or sent the item to us to photograph. Darlene Severn gets photo credit for Louise Nadeau's pieces, but it got to be too complicated to do that in each caption, so those simply say "Courtesy of Louise Nadeau." Sorry for the confusion, but we wanted to try to give photo credit where photo credit is due.

Last, but certainly not least, thanks to Johanna's friend Carolyn Cosgrove for her support and encouragement throughout this process and her always thoughtful comments.

It might also be wise to explain that Johanna did most of the writing, while Sean did many other tasks necessary to producing a book, such as contacting companies and asking for catalog pages, arranging visits to museums, factories and the patent depository, and generally being there when otherwise needed!

# Author's Note: The Peachblow Mystique

## Johanna S. Billings

I don't collect peachblow.

That might sound crazy, especially since I wrote this book at a time when many of my peers are writing books about things they collect. My first book, *Collectible Glass Rose Bowls* was about the objects of my passion. I still collect them. So, if I don't collect peachblow, whatever possessed me to write a book about it?

In a nutshell, confusion followed by fascination.

I'll never forget the first time I found myself staring peachblow in the face. Or, I should say, staring the word "peachblow" in the face. I looked into a glass case at an antique mall in Adamstown, Pennsylvania to see what I thought was a pink satin glass rose bowl. Although it was locked up, I could clearly see the $200 price tag which identified the piece as "peachblow."

I was awestruck. As a beginning collector, Sean and I developed what we called the "$35 rule." If we liked it and it was priced $35 or less, we bought it. We figured this way we could afford to collect without concerning ourselves with making expensive mistakes. I had several rose bowls like this one that I had acquired for $35 or less. What did this dealer know about this one that I didn't?

Bear in mind that as an art glass collector, I was a rank amateur. The possibility that I knew more than the dealer about this particular item was inconceivable. There had to be some minute detail that I was missing, some trick of the trade, a special key that allowed one to discern peachblow from pink satin glass. I set out to find it.

I had heard the term "peachblow" bandied about as a sort of creme de la creme in glass. The word on the street, so to speak, was that the rare and valuable peachblow glassware was what we should all aspire to collect. Trouble was, no one I talked to seemed to know just what it was we were looking for. A fellow rose bowl collector in another town was told by a dealer friend that peachblow is glass that changes color from top to bottom. In retrospect, that makes sense because peachblow is generally a heat sensitive glass, and as such it does change color from top to bottom. But that's certainly not the whole story. For us, this definition caused more confusion than clarity. Sean's grandmother acquired a rose bowl that is literally blue at the top and yellow at the bottom. Was it peachblow, we wondered?

In addition to asking people, Sean and I searched through books as our reference library grew. Some books provided a clue here or there, but none really answered the question with any thoroughness.

Meanwhile, noted Victorian glass dealer Louis O. St. Aubin, Jr. was a member of the Rose Bowl Collectors club Sean and I had founded. We could have gotten a clear and accurate answer to our burning question if we had asked him. But truth be known, we were intimidated. Louis never did anything to make us feel that way. In fact, whenever he saw us, he made a point of saying hello and remarking that he enjoyed our rose bowl newsletter. Yet we would barely grunt in response and run out of the booth for fear of embarrassing ourselves. Remember, we were beginning collectors and we knew that we didn't know very much about glass. We figured he probably realized we had a lot to learn. But we didn't want to open our mouths in front of him and remove all doubt.

Finally one day at a show, I decided I could take it no more. I had to find out what peachblow was and how to recognize it. I decided to just take a deep breath, visit Louis' booth and ask him. When I got to the booth, he wasn't there. But another guy, who I now know was Bill Pitt, was there, so I asked him. He gave me a quick lesson in peachblow 101, which covered the three major types, Mt. Washington, Wheeling and New England. No wonder there was so much confusion! Peachblow is not a single type of glassware, but a category in which there were numerous subtypes.

Having hit the mother lode of information, I promptly contacted all my confused friends and explained peachblow to them. At last, some fact had emerged from the folklore. And I was in the know. It was a wonderful feeling.

That was, of course, only the beginning. Remembering what Bill had told me required practice. *Glass Collector's Digest* had, in addition to articles on various forms of glass, advertisements from Louis in virtually every issue, and many of these ads included peachblow. Since the photos of the glass and the descriptions were on opposite pages, I used them to quiz myself by first looking at the glass, deciding if it was peachblow and if so, which type. Then I would check to see if I was right. I did the same thing with ads placed by the Burmese Cruet and Glasstiques.

Without ever intending to be, I found myself serving as a mentor to beginning collectors, showing them how to identify peachblow and referring them to ads in *Glass Collector's Digest* for further practice.

Unlike many other scholars in the antiques and collectibles field, I was actually a writer first. I thought I'd write fiction. Then I discovered glass. The rest, as they say, is history.

As my skill and confidence in identifying peachblow grew, I realized I had a golden opportunity to educate others on this misunderstood and misidentified glassware. Since I make my living writing, I could even call it "work." I've studied peachblow with a passion not unlike that of a collector, and have had a great time doing it. Making sense of the many sometimes conflicting reports is kind of like putting together the pieces of a jigsaw puzzle.

In the end, peachblow glassware turned out to be not quite as simple as those three major types. New England, Hobbs and Mt. Washington weren't the only companies bitten by the peachblow bug. Peachblow has since been produced by a number of companies, some of whose lines have little or nothing in common with those original types except the name. Hopefully, this book will help you to sort them out, so you can say with confidence that the piece before you is or isn't peachblow. More importantly, you will know why, and if it is peachblow, you will also know who made it. Hopefully you will also come to appreciate the rich and interesting history that has created the peachblow mystique.

# So Just What Is Peachblow?
# Or Is It Peach Blow?

A few sentences are all that's needed to define most terms describing glass—not so with peachblow. Or should that be "peach blow"?

First, let's address the issue of spelling. Some spell the term "peach blow" while others spell it "peachblow." Previously published reference books are divided on the spelling. That's probably due to the fact that the various companies who produced it had different spellings. We've concluded that the question of one word or two is virtually unanswerable.

The next step was to find out which term was used to describe the Chinese porcelain. Unfortunately, that only caused more confusion. In addition to both "peachblow" and "peach blow," the Chinese ware was referred to as "peachbloom" and "peach bloom." Meanwhile, Stevens & Williams called their line "Peach Bloom" while Thomas Webb & Sons called theirs "Peach Glass."

What is an author to do?

In the absence of any clear path, we chose to spell the word "peachblow" for no other reason than it's one less keystroke. We will use the word "peachblow" generically to refer to this type of glassware, no matter who produced it, and the porcelain. We will use the other spelling, and the terms "peachbloom," "peach bloom" and "peach glass" only when there is enough evidence to suggest that the particular term is, indeed, correct in that particular context, or when quoting sources directly.

Perhaps some day in the future, the question of how to spell the word will be settled. In the meantime, this seems to be the path which will yield the clearest and most consistent results.

Now, to the question of what all these terms mean. Regardless of which word you choose and how you spell it, peachblow is generally a heat-sensitive glass. That means is it a homogenous glass which gets its color change from being reheated in the glory hole, a process called "striking." The heat causes a chemical reaction which causes a color change in the portions that were heated a second time.

Of course, even that is not always true. The most well-known of the Fenton peachblow lines is a cased glass. Same with L.G. Wright (well, most of the time anyway).

There's not much that can be said that applies to all peachblow glassware. Its color, whether it's lined or one layer, whether it's decorated or not, and whether it has a matte or glossy finish all vary from manufacturer to manufacturer. That's because peachblow was really just a name, a sales gimmick, applied to not only glassware, but beauty products and pottery items as well.

This book will cover the known types of peachblow glassware in terms of what they look like and who made them, and in the last chapter, we will debunk some of the most common peachblow myths. Regardless, we are certain that readers will still eventually find a piece of glass that looks like it could be peachblow, but that doesn't fit into any of the categories discussed here. As the authors of a glass question-answer column in *AntiqueWeek*, we get numerous photos of pinkish or peachy-colored items from people wanting to know if what they have is some kind of peachblow. This happens no matter how many times we discuss what peachblow is and isn't.

Let us first refer you to the wise words of one of my predecessors, Ruth Webb Lee. In her book, *Nineteenth-Century Art Glass*, she writes, "In the face of facts, the truth should be established and the shaded 'peach' types of glass no longer labeled 'Peachblow' without regard to their original designations."

We agree. Her words lead to what is perhaps the only other general statement that can be made about peachblow.

*No matter who made it or when, peachblow gets its name from glass companies hoping to maximize public interest in their product by calling it "peachblow."*

Unlike other types of glass, the peachblow name is more important than any characteristic of the glass itself. If you can't say for certain that your item is from a line called "peachblow" by the manufacturer, then it's not peachblow, no matter what it looks like.

# Timeline

| | |
|---|---|
| **During 1885** | Thomas Webb & Sons introduces "peach glass." |
| **September 30, 1885** | Mt. Washington applies for patent for Burmese. |
| **October 3, 1885** | New England Glass Works applies for patent for its Wild Rose/peachblow. |
| **December 5, 1885** | Mt. Washington granted a patent for Burmese. |
| **March 2, 1886** | New England Glass Works granted patent for its Wild Rose/peachblow. |
| **March 8, 1886** | **MORGAN VASE SOLD** |
| **June 15, 1886** | Edward Libbey of New England Glass Works gets a patent for Plated Amberina. |
| **July 13, 1886** | New England gets a patent for Plated Wild Rose. |
| **July 20, 1886** | Mt. Washington gets trade mark on the name peachblow, securing exclusive rights to the name applied to glassware. |
| **September 2, 1886** | New England Glass Co. applies for a patent for Agata. |
| **January 18, 1887** | New England Glass Co. is granted a patent for Agata. |
| **1915** | Fenton introduces its first peachblow line, an opal glass with a pink spray applied around the top to give it color. |
| **1939** | Fenton introduces a second peachblow line, this one white outside with a pink interior casing. It lasts for one year. |
| **1940s** | Gundersen, successor to Mt. Washington, reissues peachblow using the New England formula. |
| **1940s or 50s** | Sam Diana begins making peachblow for L.G. Wright. |
| **1953** | Fenton re-introduces its peachblow coloring in hobnail. |
| **1957** | Gundersen ceases production of peachblow. |
| **January 1, 1964** | Imperial introduces a line called peachblow. |
| **1967** | Sam Diana sells his factory and peachblow formula to Harold Bennett, who produces it after hours for one or two seasons. |
| **December 31, 1967** | Imperial discontinues its line of peachblow. |
| **Late 1960s, early 1970s** | The Italians reproduce many types of Victorian glass, including peachblow. |
| **1969** | Pilgrim introduces a line called peachblow. |
| **1970** | The Kanawha Glass Co. introduces a line it calls peachblow. |
| **1970** | Pairpoint, successor to Gundersen and Gundersen-Pairpoint, resumes production of peachblow. |
| **Late 1970s** | Pilgrim ceases production of peachblow. |
| **1981** | Kanawha peachblow is phased out of their line. |
| **1988** | Pairpoint ceases production of peachblow. |
| **1993** | Intaglio introduces peachblow. |
| **Late 1990s** | Intaglio ceases production of peachblow. |
| **May 1999** | L.G. Wright goes out of business. |

MV1: The famous Morgan vase. Photo courtesy of Walters Art Gallery.

# ❦ CHAPTER 1 ❦

# The Morgan Vase

Walking up the front steps to the Walters Art Gallery for the first time, I felt like I'd discovered the proverbial pot of gold at the end of the rainbow. After all, I was about to see the vase that made history, not just with its own shining moment more than 100 years ago, but for collectors today.

Wow. That's some impact.

"It's nothing much," I'd been told. Sure, I guess it's nothing much when compared to a Thomas Webb satin rose bowl with Jules Barbe enameling or a piece of Mt. Washington Crown Milano. Still, it has a certain presence. It's an attractive piece. But I found myself far more captivated by its history than its looks.

Naturally, I'm talking about the so-called "Morgan vase," a Chinese porcelain piece that sold at auction for $18,000 in March 1886, starting the Victorian peachblow craze.

The Morgan vase has not changed hands since the auction, when it was purchased by William and Henry Walters. In fact, it's currently on display at the Walters Art Gallery in Baltimore, along with about 20 additional pieces of Chinese porcelain peachblow. Walters was by no means a publicity hound and purchased the vase unaware that a media circus would follow, in which the vase would become a symbol of excess and extravagance.

Despite the varied opinions of his day, Walters knew what he was doing. The famous vase bears the six-character K'ang Hsi mark, which means it was produced during this emperor's reign, between 1662 and 1722. More importantly, the eight shapes to bear this mark are the only Chinese porcelains known to have been produced in limited quantities. All eight shapes were intended for use on the writing tables of emperors, nobles and scholars and are known as the "Eight Great Numbers." (see illustrations, page 12)

The shape of the Morgan vase is known in China as a "three string vase," a name which refers to the three thin, string-like bands around the base of its neck. The width and spacing of the three "strings" are similar to those found on Chinese musical instruments.

The eight-piece table set also includes the "coiled dragon vase," which is similar in shape to the Morgan vase, but with a coiled dragon around the neck. A third shape, the "Kuan Yin Vase" or "amphora vase," has a similar, but thinner and less majestic shape, and is smaller. The "Lotus Petal Vase" is about the same height as the Morgan vase, but has a more globular bottom and a longer neck. The bottom half of the globular base is ribbed. What these pieces were used for is unclear. Perhaps they were intended to hold writing utensils or flowers or maybe they were simply decorative.

The fifth piece is known in America as the "writer's semi-globular water coup," but is known in China as the "chicken coop vase" because the shape resembles bamboo baskets used there to house chickens. It is domed with a small protruding neck and three coiled dragon medallions spaced equidistant around the body. Writers used this vase as a container for water into which they would dip their brushes, using the neck of the vase to shape the tips of their brushes as desired.

The "apple-shaped vase" or "writer's apple-shaped water coup" was used in a similar manner to the chicken coop vase. However, this piece is somewhat smaller and has no neck, but rather a bowl-sized opening.

The "gong-shaped washer" or "writer's brush bath" is a shallow bowl with a wide opening used to clean brushes. The eighth item in the set, known as the "seal color box" resembles a covered trinket box, the lid and base being about the same size. It was used to hold ink paste.

Peachblow porcelain items produced during the K'ang Hsi reign are reputed to be the finest specimens of peachblow porcelain ever produced.

*MV2: The K'ang Hsi mark on the bottom of the Morgan vase. Photo courtesy of Walters Art Gallery.*

Oddly, however, the color of Chinese porcelain peachblow Morgan vase is really closer to that of Agata art glass than any line of peachblow. The vase is a rich pink, with some slightly mottled areas, and a white interior. When Hobbs, Brockunier & Co. did its facsimile of the Morgan vase in what we now call Wheeling peachblow, the company got the size and shape right, but not the color. But then again, this line, originally called "Coral," wasn't intended to imitate the color of the vase at all. (See Chapter 3.)

Peachblow porcelains are as varied in color as peachblow glassware. Like the glassware, most peachblow porcelains are not the least bit peachy in color. Most are some shade of red or brownish red, and sometimes even are marked with flecks of green! Most of the time, the surface of these porcelains is somewhat mottled, with several color nuances apparent in a single piece. The differences in color have to do with the glaze and manufacturing

***MV3****: Six of the eight shapes found bearing the K'ang Hsi mark and known as the "Eight Great Numbers." Back: from left, the lotus petal vase, the three string vase (Morgan vase), and the amphora vase. Front: Chicken coop vase, gong-shaped washer or writer's brush bath, and seal color box. Note that you cannot see the coiled dragon medallion usually found on the chicken coop vase. Not shown are the coiled dragon vase and the apple-shaped vase. Photo courtesy of Walters Art Gallery.*

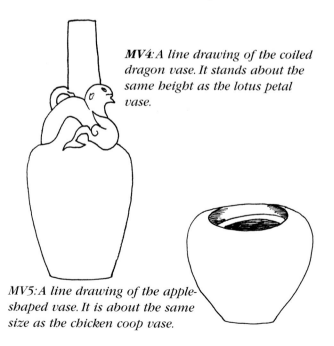

*MV4: A line drawing of the coiled dragon vase. It stands about the same height as the lotus petal vase.*

*MV5: A line drawing of the apple-shaped vase. It is about the same size as the chicken coop vase.*

process, which we won't attempt to explain here. Regardless, it seems rather fitting that a porcelain of varying color should inspire lines of glassware whose colors are as varied.

There's no doubt that the vase was, indeed, a treasure. Nevertheless, William and Henry Walters' purchase created a media frenzy akin to those surrounding a major scandal. Some of the reason for this seems to be the fact that Chinese porcelains were not widely known or collected in America.

The vase had been part of a collection belonging to New York resident Mary Jane Morgan, widow of shipping magnate Charles Morgan. Despite her apparent wealth, she lived a frugal life until her husband's death in 1878. She then began indulging herself with exotic flowers, jewelry and art. When she died seven years later, she had a considerable collection.

It should be pointed out that Mrs. Morgan was no relation to J.P. Morgan, an American transportation millionaire who owned the White Star Line (which owned the *Titanic*), among other things.

The first time the vase was mentioned in the press was in October 1885, when the *Art Amateur* reported that Mrs. Morgan had paid $15,000 for it.

Mary Morgan's estate was sold by Thomas F. Kirby of the American Art Association in 12 sales held over 10 days, beginning March 3, 1886. Kirby wanted the auction to be a social event, rather than simply a commercial one, and promoted the event with a fancy no-holds-barred catalog. Perhaps due in part to the earlier mention in *Art Amateur*, the now-famous vase, which was lot 341 of the sale, seemed to capture the public's attention from the very beginning. The catalog describes it as follows: "Vase of graceful ovoid shape with slender neck slightly spreading at top, perfection in form, color and texture. Height exclusive of carved stand, 8 inches, diameter 3 inches. Mark of the Kang-he (sic) period, 1661-1722. The above from the private collection of I Wang-Ye, a Mandarin Prince, has a worldwide reputation as being the finest specimen of its class in existence."

When the sale opened, William Walters was there, successfully bidding $7,100 for a watercolor painting titled *The Rare Vase* by artist Mariano Fortuny y Marsal. It showed an eighteenth-century connoisseur posed next to a large famille rose vase on a rococo stand. (see illustration on page 16)

Walters had returned to Baltimore by the time the now-famous vase crossed the block. However, his son Henry was there. A report of the sale, quoted by Albert Christian Revi in an article in the January-February 1965 issue of *Spinning Wheel* reads as follows:

Meanwhile the attendant, solemn as a sphinx, was taking from its wrappings in a box the $15,000 vase, which was the first piece offered. There was a moment's hush until "$5,000" from someone in the rear broke the stillness. This was rapidly increased, $1,000 at a time until $13,000 had been reached. Here Mr. Crocker, who had been giving his bids with his eyelids as fast as he could wink, dropped out. There was no cessation in the war until $15,000, Mrs. Morgan's purchase price, was reached, when a round of applause interrupted Mr. Kirby. Then the price bid was increased by hundreds until Mr. Walters paralyzed the other bidder by his offer of $18,000.

Interestingly, William Johnston, a curator at the Walters Art Gallery, writes in the book *William and Henry Walters* that James Sutton bid on behalf of an undisclosed client. Since Revi doesn't say when the article he quotes was published or where, it's not clear whether the writer knew Sutton was bidding on Walters' behalf or whether he found this out later.

Several other peachblow porcelain items were sold at the same auction, though these did not attract the attention of the public or the press. As described by Ruth Webb Lee in *Nineteenth-Century Art Glass*, these other items are an ovoid vase, 8.5" tall, $1200; an amphora shaped vase (probably a "Kuan Yin Vase"), 6" high, $1,150; an ovoid vase 8.25" high (possibly a "Lotus Petal Vase"), $1,000, and a semi-globular bottle vase (probably a "chick-

*MV6: Henry Walters. Photo courtesy of Walters Art Gallery.*

*MV7: William Walters. Photo courtesy of Walters Art Gallery.*

en coop vase"), $675.

The day after the sale of the now famous vase, William Walters denied to the Baltimore press that he had purchased the vase. A *Baltimore Sun* reporter quoted him as saying, "The idea that I should pay $18,000 for a vase is ridiculous. I neither bought it, nor did anyone buy it for me, nor did I buy it for anyone else."

However, Henry Walters authorized Sutton to tell the truth. "I wish it was understood, once and for all, that I bought the vase for Mr. W. T. Walters," Sutton is quoted as saying. "When it reaches its destination, as it will in a few days, I trust that the Baltimore papers will no longer prevaricate about it … There are not more than forty of its kind in existence, and it is no doubt the finest specimen."

Walters' denial of the purchase caused the *Baltimore Sun* to speculate that the Art Society, which had sold the vase to Mrs. Morgan, had purchased it and rumors to that effect ran rampant.

Back in New York City, the *New York Times* reported the following in its March 9, 1886 edition:

> The greatest excitement was when the famous $18,000 Peachblow vase was set on the table covered with a spread of old gold cloth. To any but a connoisseur it appeared to be a very common bit of plain porcelain. Ovoid in shape, it had a slender neck, spreading slightly at the top. It was three inches in diameter and eight inches in height. I Wang-Ye, a Chinese Mandarin Prince, once owned it. That was one point in its favor. It was made in the Tang-He (sic) period, somewhere between 1661 and 1722, and that was another point. Its peculiar color, that of a peach blossom, was a perfect reproduction of that peculiar tint, which is so difficult to obtain. It was this feature that set collectors to raving; and the experts among them say it was the finest specimen of its class in existence. A sharp rivalry for its possession was anticipated; but the price it brought exceeded all expectations.

A subsequent article in the *Times*, which ran on March 24, created a stir by exposing many of the claims surrounding this vase to be fraudulent. "The vase was never in the collection of I Wang-Ye, who is called 'Mandarin Prince,'" reads the article. "There are, in China, Mandarins, who are Government Officials, and Princes, who are of royal blood. But a Mandarin doesn't become a Prince except in art sale catalogues." Addressed to "collectors generally, and to Mr. William T. Walters particularly," the article goes on to say that the vase wasn't even an authentic peachblow, according to an unnamed authority who claimed that R. Austin Robertson, from the American Art Association, had purchased the vase in Peking the previous year for 250 Mexican silver dollars. The article suggests that the high price paid by Mrs. Morgan was caused by a clerk who misread the price tag.

Interestingly, this article claims the price had been $200 and that the clerk misread the tag as $2,000. Yet it was well documented that Mrs. Morgan paid $15,000. Where these crazy figures came from is a mystery.

Those who visited the Walters Art Gallery after the sale failed to find the famous vase. Revi's *Spinning Wheel* article states that the vase was stored in a vault for 50 years due to the unpleasant publicity surrounding its purchase. However, Johnston says that Walters probably simply removed the carved wooden stand and put the vase

on display with others of the same color.

On March 27, 1886, the *Times* poked fun at the peachblow craze by publishing *The Rime of the Peachblow Vase*, a parody of Samuel Taylor Coleridge's *The Rime of the Ancient Mariner*. Other publications took their shots as well. The *Philadelphia News* ran the *Ballade of the Peach Blow Vase*. A contemporary article in the *Crockery and Glass Journal* had this to say:

> There was plenty of bad taste displayed in the purchase of bric-a-brac; we might say foolishness…Just try to imagine, if you can, porcelains, cameo glass, plaques, bronzes, from all parts of the world, for which one million and a half of the old man Morgan's money was paid, rammed into one private house. Fancy a lone widow with a moderate family having 'bung' after 'bung' of the finest plates ever made. Numbers of these plates cost more than their weight in gold, some of them double that, but they will never bring it at auction unless someone is as insane as Mrs. Morgan.
>
> Then there is that $15,000 vase. What a big fraud it is, or rather, small fraud for big bait…It is without a doubt the nastiest looking argillaceous chestnut we remember to have seen. The *New York Sun* very wisely descants upon its merits and says, "There is not now enough inventive genius in the world to duplicate it or any like piece of porcelain!" Bah! Who would want to duplicate it? We will venture to say that if any modern potter could duplicate it, even with its skin-disease glaze, he could not sell it for ten cents.
>
> People who had not seen it were crowding around on the last day of the exhibition, and solid ranks of crockery crazy women were expressing their rapturous admiration for this sickly little bottle with a battered neck. We were disappointed in this awfully costly plug-ugly of ceramic art, and did not hesitate to say so. We had but one sympathizer, a newspaperman, and he agreed exactly…

### Ballade of the Peach Blow Vase
#### from the *Philadelphia News*, 1886

No "crimson-tippet flower"
Formed from Columbian earth,
No creature of an hour—
Of centuries I am the birth.
All else is little worth
Beside my ancient race!
Come, moderate your mirth;
I am the Peach-blow vase!

Of Khang Hy there's a dearth;
The jealous Western Giaour
Ou-tsai-khi on his hearth
To polish lacks the power.
They glow alone to dower
Princesses who may trace
Blood to which Mandarin

cower:
I am the Peach-blow vase!
Give me a fitting girth,
Let Baltimore come vow her
Leal as the Maid of Perth,
And build a pearly bower!
So that when critics sour
Come pilgrims to my grace,
In all my pride I'll tower;
I am the Peach-blow vase!

Envoy
When gazing on my face:
I'm made of kiln-dried flour—
I am the Peach-blow vase!
—- J.P.B.

## The Rime of the Peachblow Vase
### from the New York Times, March 27, 1886

It is an ancient connoisseur,
And he stoppeth one of three,
And saith, "Now hearken while I tell
A tale of Ou-tsai-khi."

"Now, by our lady," whispers one,
"He hath a gruesome gaze."
"Oh, hark!" quoth he, "and list to me;
I tell of a peachblow vase."

"In the Yang-khi time, some ages back.
My tale it doth begin,
When Spring was fair in the flowery land
And the town of King-te-chin.

There was an aged potterer—
A worshipper of the sun;
I tell about a wonderous vase,
By home one day begun.

He molded it with loving hand,
And fashioned it with care,
And said 'This vase shall all excel;
None with it shall compare.'

Its body round and swelling was,
Its neck was long and thin,
Its shoulder's curve was exquisite—
This vase of King-te-chin.

Then rose this ancient potterer,
And said with exultation:
'This rare and radiant vase shall be
For imperial delectation.'

No vase like this on earth or deep
Posterity shall see;
Its fame shall grow eternally
As sure as it's Tohang-khi.

Around its sacred form the fire
Shall slowly upward reach,
And all its face shall blush and glow
With rare bloom of the peach.

Then three times round the old man went,
And three times round he went;
And winked his eye and scratched his ear,
And poked his fire with glee.

But o'er the silent purple sea
Up rose a cloudlike mass,
And from it came a pure white squall
Of a very superior class.

This squall it fanned the sacred fire
Until it grew too hot,
And brought upon that good old man
A most unhappy lot.

For when the work should have been done
Upon that wonderous vase,
The old man's heart was filled quite full
Of wonder and amaze.

He beat his breast and loud he wailed:
'I would that I were dead!'
My vase has te'en no peachblow tint,
But a third-rate strawberry red.

'Alas, alack, and well-a-day!
Unhappy that I am;
Instead of being a priceless thing,
It is not worth a—clam!'

Then down he went to the sounding sea,
And standing by the shore,
The vase threw far o'er the harbor bar,
And saw it nevermore.

But a fisherman dropped a big brown net
Just where that vase fell in,
And hauled it out with a lot of fish,
And took it to Pekin.

And when he sold his smelts and eels,
(Not knowing of King-te-chin)
He said to a buyer who liked the vase,
'I'll chuck the blamed thing in.'

And so this man took home the vase,
Accepted in a minute;
He places it on his toilet stand,
And kept his cue grease in it.

The years passed on, the man passed off,
And the vase from King-te-chin
Was snapped up by a peddling chap,
Who lived in West Pekin.

And over and over and over again
That strawberry vase was sold;
But never a time in the flowery clime
Was it worth its weight in gold.

For in those days a strawberry vase
Was no better than a blue,
As all men knew, from a peddler up
To the Emperor Wun-Foo-Foo.

A couple of centuries glided by,
And then a Western sage,
Who'd crossed two oceans in search of
notions,
Suspected the vase's age.

And he said to the man who owned it then—
A mandarin big-bug,
With a snake like cue and parchment face—
'How much'll you take for your jug?'

The mandarin shook his bullet head,
And said:'He muchee old;
He nice Tchange-yao from King-te-chin;
He fetchee big heap of gold.'

The Western sage then softly smiles
As the mandarin's back he pats,
And says:'I'll give you a hundred dollars:'
The mandarin says:'Oh, rats!'

The Western sage, in course of time,
The mandarin did pay
Two hundred and fifty Mexican dollars,
And took the jug away.

Across the oceans, to dealers in notions,
The little red jug then crossed!
And they sold it off at a slight advance
Of fifty times its cost!

But alas! the god, who sent the squall
That blew the maker's blaze,
Had sent along a curse so strong
That it burned into the vase.

And so it chanced that this red jug,
Of diminutive dimensions,
Will always be a fruitful source
Of very grave dissensions."

Then three times round went the connoisseur,
And three times round went he;
And he blow his nose and dropped a tear,
And sank to the bottom of the sea.

And I verily believe since I heard this tale,
With sorrow and amaze,
That the one who told it, with smirk and grin,
Was the ghost—from the town of King-te-
chin—
Of the man who made the vase.

*MV8: Painting, The Rare Vase by artist Mariano Fortuny y Marsal. William Walters paid $7,100 for this watercolor painting on March 3, 1886 the day the Morgan estate sale opened. Photo courtesy of Walters Art Gallery.*

Cartoonists and gag writers also got laughs at the expense of "the crazy Widow Morgan" and her "plug-ugly of ceramic art."

"'A peachblow vase was knocked down for $18,000,' read Mrs. Diggory," goes one gag in an 1887 edition of *Western Farmer's Almanac.* "'My gracious alive! Why, I would have knocked it down for 75 cents if I didn't have to pay for it in case it broke when it fell.'"

The furor actually lasted for years. The Dec. 5, 1894 issue of *New York Commercial Advertiser* claimed Charles Dana, owner of the *New York Sun* and himself a collector of Chinese porcelains, had actually been the buyer. Not only had the *Sun* championed the vase while the *Times* belittled it, but also, the *Advertiser* maintained, only someone insane enough to pay $18,000 for a single vase would support the type of governmental defense spending supported by the *Sun.*

Adverse publicity may have embarrassed Walters, but it did little to snuff out the peachblow fire that burned in this country. B.D. Baldwin & Co. of Chicago released a line of beauty products under the trade name "Peach Blow" and women were not considered to be in fashion without peachblow coloring on their cheeks and lips. The line included perfumes, cosmetics, sachet powders, dentifrices and hair dressings.

L. Strauss & Sons, wholesale distributors of imported glass and china, carried pottery facsimiles probably made in Bohemia, some with enameled floral decorations. Their ad, run in three trade publications, reads:

> The Famous Peach Blow Vase and other Novelties ... We have at last succeeded in securing a fac-simile of the famous Peach Blow Vase, which was recently sold at the Morgan sale for $18,000. This reproduction is in pottery, the same as the original, and is exact as to size, shape, as well as color, and has been pronounced by competent critics as the only successful reproduction of the peculiar shade of color known as Crushed Strawberry, which made the original such a rare specimen of Chinese art. This color is peculiar to pottery and cannot be reproduced in glass. Aside from the intrinsic value of this fac-simile Vase, and its salableness, it will serve as a most attractive advertisement by reason of the extraordinary notoriety which the original had gained. Our price for the vase and stand is $24.00 a dozen net.

The glass industry was probably the most prolific producer of peachblow facsimiles, at least by name. "A new craze in glassware has been developed. As might have been expected, it is anything in 'peach-blow' color, caused by the public interest aroused in the celebrated vase from the Morgan collection," reports the April 29, 1886 issue of *Pottery and Glassware Reporter.* "On the counters and shelves of glassware dealers are beginning to be seen all shades of the 'peach-blow' and it is prophesied that it will spread over nearly every article of ornamental crockery."

Three major American glassmakers jumped on the peachblow bandwagon. Interestingly, all three of the lines now known as "peachblow" were either already in production or projected at the time the Morgan vase was sold. It seems the companies simply capitalized on the name, much as stuffed toy manufacturers today use the word "beanie." Each of those stories will be told in the following chapters, along with the stories of the many firms to capitalize on the name "peachblow" since 1886. Even if Mary Morgan was crazy, her legacy has lasted more than a century and inspired a variety of different lines in glassware. These are the many faces of peachblow.

> **TRIVIA:** The Peachblow, Colorado post office was open from 1890 until 1909. Because the post office closed, the town no longer officially exists.

**WE1B: The back of the vase is decorated with a butterfly. Photo by Bill Pitt, courtesy of Brookside Antiques.**

**WE1A: It would make sense that a line called "Peach Glass" would be colored like this vase. Photo by Bill Pitt, courtesy of Brookside Antiques.**

# Webb, Stevens & Williams and Carder Steuben Peachblow

Since it's difficult to discuss the development of peach-blow glassware without discussing Thomas Webb & Sons' "Peach Glass," this seemed to be the best place to start. Unfortunately, very little is documented in the United States concerning Webb's Peach Glass, leaving collectors to guess at the shapes produced, decorations and exact coloring. Even books on British glass by British authors generally do not include more than a sentence or two referring to British peachblow. Here's what we have been able to find out.

Webb introduced "Peach Glass" in 1885. It is not known exactly when it came out, but Webb pattern books—original company records of the lines, shapes and decorations produced—list "peach mat" and "peach iridescent" vases on Nov. 11, 1885. A 7.5" "peach bloom vase" is also noted, which might explain why many people refer to Webb peachblow as "peach bloom."

Webb's Peach Glass was described that same year in *The Pottery Gazette*, a British trade journal, as, "a delicate blend of colour shaded so as to resemble a peach."

British Author H.W. Woodward gives us a small clue in his book *Art, Feat and Mystery: The Story of Thomas Webb & Sons, Glassmakers* when he writes, "Early in 1886, flint decoration was being applied to the peach body and peach was being blown in a diamond mould to produce a 6-inch bowl with a flint stem and 'ivory' flowers. Another glass to be used with peach was topaz." It would appear that peach glass items were produced with applied glass decorations, or that peach glass was simply one color used in tandem with other colors to create the finished article.

Charles R. Hajdamach, author of *British Glass: 1800-1914*, says that Plated Amberina, patented by Joseph Locke on behalf of the New England Glass Works, was "virtually identical" to Webb's Peach Glass. He goes on to say that Plated Amberina, Webb's Peach Glass and the "'Peach Blow' version made by American factories" were identical to Locke's product in terms of manufacturing process—a heat sensitive layer of glass cased with a creamy white layer. Hajdamach doesn't say which of the American factories he refers to, but the fact that he compares the Webb product to Plated Amberina seems to indicate that he was referring to the Hobbs line.

Hajdamach's comment and the quote from *The Pottery Gazette* make it sound as if Webb's Peach Glass shades from a rich mahogany red to yellowish orange, much like the Hobbs line we know as "Wheeling peachblow." If that's the case, then one could argue that the shaded red to pink cased glassware often sold in this country as Webb peachblow is not, in fact, from the company's Peach Glass line.

***WE2: The color of this little vase is a bit darker than is typically found, but it certainly resembles the color of a peach.***

*WE3: This Webb punch cup is peachblow because it shades from a rich red to a peachy color. The Severn Collection.*

*WE3A: The pontil area on Webb pieces often show a cross section of the glass. You can definitely see here that the base of the outer layer of glass is peach colored, not pink or white.*

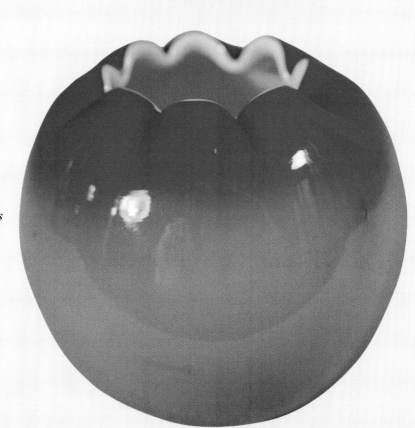

*WE4: This miniature rose bowl also shows the peach hue. Photo by Bill Pitt, courtesy of Brookside Antiques.*

**WE5:** *The decorated rose bowl on the left, with Jules Barbe enameling, is definitely peach colored. The undecorated one on the right appears rose to pink by comparison, but does actually have a peach hue in the outer layer of glass. Authors' collection.*

**WE6:** *Note the butterfly on the back of the Jules Barbe decorated rose bowl.*

**WE7:** *This photo shows the Webb pontil mark on the undecorated rose bowl in the photo above. It reveals a cross section of layers of glass. The subtle peach hue is a little more evident here.*

**WE8:** *The peach hue is subtle, but there, in this pair of Jules Barbe decorated Webb vases shown both front and back. The Severn Collection.*

*WE9: A small rose bowl, this one on three toes. Again, it's subtle, but the peach hue is definitely there. Collection of Ruth Sparks.*

ments at the Corning Museum of Glass note that the Stevens & Williams line is shaded pink glass with a white interior. We were able to photograph a shoulder vase, in a color very similar to the glass usually referred to as Webb peachblow, only it has a Stevens & Williams mark. It makes at least as much sense to call this vase peachblow as to call either of the other two color combinations peachblow, at least without further documentation.

In light of how much we don't know or can't prove, it would seem prudent to exercise caution when declaring a piece to be either Webb Peach Glass or Stevens & Williams Peach Bloom.

Since the name Frederick Carder is thought of in close association with Stevens & Williams, this seemed to be the best place to mention Carder Steuben Peachblow. In 1928, Steuben produced small quantities of a glass it called peachblow for the Crest Company. Steuben made two shapes, a lamp base and a vase, both designated as 8571. In 1928, the wholesale cost would have been $2.50 per piece. The glass actually looks more like Burmese, shading from a rose pink to golden sulphur yellow.

Currently in this country, Webb peachblow is identified as the red to orange, red or pink shaded to peach, or as darker pink shading to lighter pink. Most collectors and dealers seem certain they're correct, regardless of which coloration they refer to as Webb peachblow, but they're generally unable to say *how* they know they're correct.

It's important to say that a definitive answer on the coloration is not possible. However, the available evidence suggests that a rose to peach coloring is correct and a pink to white coloring it not. We believe that pink to lighter pink or pink to white glass with a white interior layer is cased glass, nothing more.

This section includes photos of what we believe to be Webb Peach Glass. Some of the peach hues are quite subtle. Others are not. For the sake of comparison, we are including photos of Webb pink cased glass, but those photos are found in the last chapter, which covers items that are not peachblow. That way, it will be less confusing.

If information on Webb's Peach Glass is sketchy, then Stevens & Williams "Peach Bloom" is almost completely obscure. The little that does exist is contradictory. The book *Frederick Carder and His Steuben Glass* by Thomas P. Dimitroff shows a photo of a shaded brown to amber Mat-su-no-ke rose bowl identified as Stevens & Williams peachblow. Research docu-

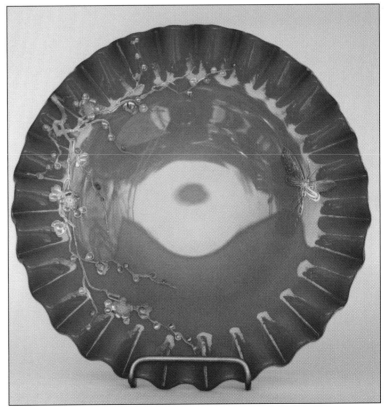

*WE10: The peach hue is not so subtle on this plate. The Severn Collection.*

*WE12: This Webb peachblow vase has a subtle peach hue. Courtesy of Brookside Antiques.*

*WE11: Webb peachblow cracker jar with Jules Barbe enameling and butterfly on back. The peach hue is subtle but definitely there. The Severn Collection.*

**WE13: The dragon decoration is unusual on this vase, deemed to be peachblow because of the subtle peach hue. Photo courtesy of Barbara Loudon.**

**WE14:** *A Miniature Webb peachblow egg-shaped rose bowl with an applied clear foot. Collection of Stu Horn.*

**S&W1:** *This vase is signed "Stevens & Williams" in a circular mark which is raised, similar to a notary seal. Is it Peach Bloom? It certainly has a peachy cast to it. But the truth is, no documentation on Stevens & Williams Peach Bloom has surfaced in the United States.*

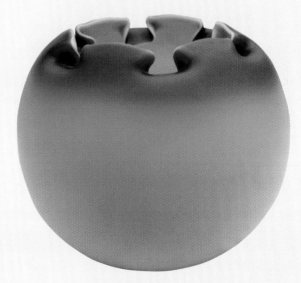

**WE15:** *This Webb peachblow piece is unusual because of the applied amber base. Its shape is much like the one above, except the top doesn't turn in. The Severn Collection.*

**S&W3:** *This Stevens & Williams rose bowl is the same color as the Mat-su-no-ke piece identified as Stevens & Williams peachblow in the book* Frederick Carder and His Steuben Glass. *Is it Peach Bloom? We don't know. Authors' collection.*

## Webb Peachblow Identification Card

**Proper Name:** Peach Glass.
**Manufacturer:** Thomas Webb & Sons, Stourbridge, England.
**Date of Production:** Introduced around 1885. How long it was produced is unknown.
**Color:** Shades from deep red rose to golden orange, or rose pink to peach.
**Casing:** Yes, creamy white.
**Finish:** Both matte and glossy.
**Decorations:** Often found with Jules Barbe gold floral enameling. Butterflies, bees and other insects are often present.
**Special Characteristics:** Pontil is polished and generally shows a cross section of the layers of glass. Be sure not to confuse Webb Peach Glass with cased pink or pink to white glass, which is often found with Jules Barbe decorations. Also, be sure not to confuse Webb Peach Glass with a similar product made by the Harrach firm of Bohemia, discussed in Chapter 17.

## Stevens & Williams Peachblow Identification Card

**Proper Name:** Peach Bloom.
**Manufacturer:** Stevens & Williams of Brierley Hill, England.
**Date of Production:** Unknown.
**Color:** Unknown. Reported to be shaded pink or to peach, pink to white, or brown to amber, depending on whom you consult.
**Casing:** Probably cased in white, but even this is really unknown.
**Finish:** Unknown.
**Decorations:** Unknown.
**Special Characteristics:** Unknown.

## Carder Steuben Peachblow Identification Card

**Proper Name:** Peachblow.
**Manufacturer:** Steuben Glass Works, Corning, NY.
**Date of Production:** 1928.
**Color:** Shades from rose pink to sulphur yellow.
**Casing:** None.
**Finish:** Both matte and glossy.
**Decorations:** None.
**Special Characteristics:** The production was so small that finding a genuine piece is unlikely.

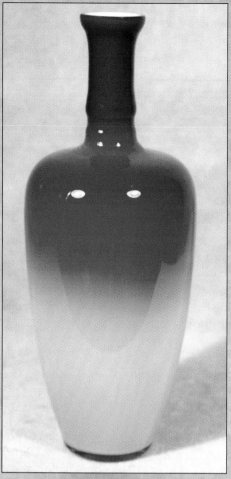

**WH1: Hobbs' facsimile of the famous Morgan vase, shown without its stand, is shape No. 22 in their catalog. Photo by Bill Pitt, courtesy of Brookside Antiques.**

**WH1A & WH1B: The pressed amber stand made to go with the Morgan vase and the two shown together. Photos by Bill Pitt, courtesy of Brookside Antiques.**

# CHAPTER 3

# Wheeling Peachblow

Regardless of what Webb's Peach Glass actually looks like, it played an important part in the development of peachblow lines in America. Apparently, the line we now know as Wheeling peachblow was copied from Webb. The *Wheeling Daily Intelligencer* newspaper had this to say in September 1886: "When Thomas Webb, of England, made his first shipment of coral, or peachblow ware, to New York, Mr. Wm. Leighton, Jr., secured a piece of the ware and before the second shipment had been opened in New York, the always enterprising firm was turning out the same ware, which is being sold by some dealers as imported goods."

The article doesn't say when Leighton nabbed his sample of Webb's Peach Glass, but we do know that Coral was in the works because the company had been promoting it in 1885. The Nov. 26, 1885 issue of the *American Pottery and Glassware Reporter* says, "Among their (Hobbs') latest novelties is the Coral ware, which for elegance of shape and beauty of coloring cannot be excelled anywhere. They have a line of pitchers in this ware of exquisite finish, the colors rivaling the bloom on the peach.... They are making many fancy articles in antique styles modeled from pieces taken from ancient ruins."

The Dec. 3, 1885 edition of the *American Pottery and Glassware Reporter* announces Hobbs' "newest and in many respects most beautiful Coral ware, which will be ready for sale January 1, 1886."

The company often referred to the line in trade journals as "Coral, sometimes called Peach Blow." The Nov. 25, 1886 edition of *Crockery & Glass Journal* implies that when Coral was given a matte finish, it was peachblow: "At Hobbs, Brockunier and Co.'s trade is excellent. The demand for their lustreless coral, known to the trade as peachblow, is beyond expectations, and keeps up remarkably well. The firm is now making tasty holiday goods. Pears, peaches and other fruits in coral, richly tinted, look good enough to eat."

According to a January 1962 magazine article, "Wheeling Peach Blow and Rainbow Mother of Pearl Satin" by H. Ogden Wintermute, William Leighton, Jr., working for Hobbs, actually intended to duplicate the color of the Morgan vase when creating the company's Coral line. This doesn't fit with other known facts, however. It is entirely possible that Leighton went to New York to examine and measure the Morgan vase so that Hobbs could reproduce the shape. If Leighton intended to reproduce the color of the Morgan vase in Hobbs' glass, he failed miserably.

Hobbs' contemporaries recognized that the firm did an excellent job copying the shape of the vase. "The best imitation of the famous $18,000 Morgan vase is manufactured by this firm, and although the first imitation was put on the market early this spring, the sales have been enormous and the

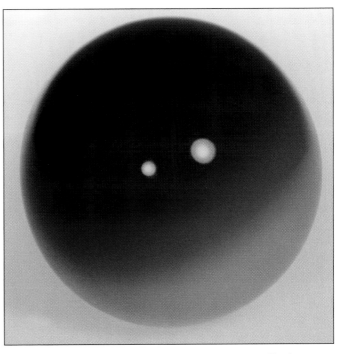

**WH2:** *A scarce Wheeling peachblow witch's ball. Photo courtesy of Oglebay Institute.*

demand for them is on the increase," reads one trade journal article. Plus, the company's glassware included a white lining, not unlike the inside of the vase. The color of the outer layer of glass is completely different, however, which supports the argument that the company did not make its Coral/Peachblow line to imitate the Morgan vase, but simply began using the name "peachblow" and later added the Morgan vase shape to the line.

Copies of the Morgan vase, which came with a pressed amber stand designed to imitate the wooden stand with the original, sold quite well, according to sales reports in *Crockery and Glass Journal* in 1886 and 1887. The matte finish appears to have been more popular than glossy.

One can't help but notice the similarities between Hobbs' Coral and Plated Amberina, made by the New England Glass Works, and patented June 15, 1886. Plated Amberina looks virtually identical to Wheeling peachblow, except that Plated Amberina has vertical ribs molded in the glass and Wheeling peachblow does not. The lining in Plated Amberina is opalescent, sometimes with a very subtle bluish cast. The lining on Wheeling peachblow is definitely white and is not opalescent. Since Plated Amberina was not called Peachblow when it was originally made, it is not Peachblow and is not included here.

*WH3: This bulbous jack-in-the-pulpit is the only piece of Wheeling peachblow known to be lined in any color but white. Photo courtesy of Oglebay Institute.*

*WH4: A Wheeling peachblow parlor lamp would be a real treasure to have. But you're not very likely to find one. Photo courtesy of Oglebay Institute.*

*WH5: These vases are the only known examples of spangled Wheeling peachblow. They were donated to Oglebay by the Frohme estate. Mr. Frohme was head of sales at Hobbs. Photo courtesy of Oglebay Institute.*

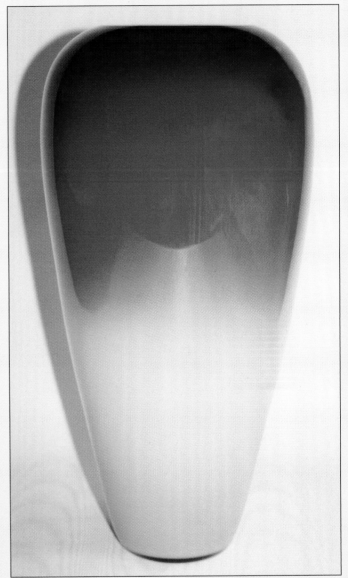

**WH6**: This Wheeling peachblow ovoid vase is quite large, standing about 20" tall. This shape comes in four different sizes and is designated in the catalog as No. 19, No. 18, No. 17 or No. 23, depending on the height. The largest size is the rarest.

**WH8**: The No. 6 vase in matte. Photo by Bill Pitt, courtesy of Brookside Antiques.

**WH11:** *If you take the No. 11 vase, left, and add a band of applied rigaree, you get what was referred to in Hobbs catalogs as the No. 12 vase.*

Both lines were manufactured in the same way, yet no record can be found of any dispute or argument between the two companies over patent infringements. Some authors have surmised that the companies may have reached an agreement on these lines when Hobbs was licensed to produce Amberina under the Libbey patent. However, Hobbs was licensed to produce Amberina in February 1886, four months prior to the development of Plated Amberina. Still, it's possible that the two firms worked out an agreement on this ware. If the licensing of Amberina was a success, New England may have decided it was in its best interests not to get in an uproar over Coral, assuming, of course, that Plated Amberina came before Coral. (We know Plated Amberina was patented June 15, 1886, and obviously it had been in the works before that date. We don't know exactly when Coral was developed.) Or, perhaps the lack of opalescence in the Hobbs line was how they got around the Libbey patent.

---

### Wheeling Peachblow Identification Card

**Proper Name:** Coral, but the line was often referred to by the manufacturer as "Peachblow" or "Peach Blow." Some trade journal references seem to indicate that "Peachblow" or "Peach Blow" were the names used for the matte finish while Coral was the proper name for the glossy finish.

**Manufacturer:** Hobbs, Brockunier & Co., Wheeling, WV.

**Date of Production:** First available to the public on Jan. 1, 1886. It's unknown exactly how long it was produced, but reports indicate it sold well through 1895.

**Color:** Shades from deep mahogany red to golden orange-yellow.

**Casing:** Yes, off-white.

**Finish:** Both matte and glossy.

**Decorations:** Sometimes found with applied amber rigaree. Handles and stoppers are also made of amber glass.

**Special Characteristics:** Beware if the pontil is not polished. And beware of Italian reproductions. (See Chapter 9.)

**WH9**: *The double gourd vase was Hobbs No. 7 vase in catalogs. Photo by Bill Pitt, courtesy of Brookside Antiques.*

**WH10**: *The double gourd vase in matte.*

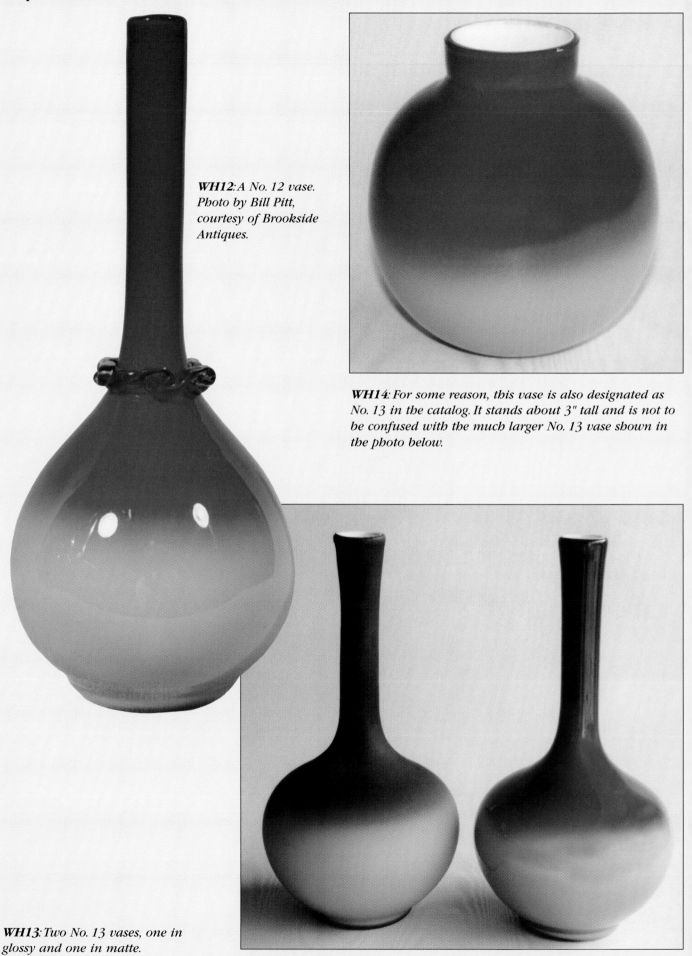

**WH12**: A No. 12 vase.
Photo by Bill Pitt,
courtesy of Brookside
Antiques.

**WH14**: For some reason, this vase is also designated as
No. 13 in the catalog. It stands about 3" tall and is not to
be confused with the much larger No. 13 vase shown in
the photo below.

**WH13**: Two No. 13 vases, one in
glossy and one in matte.

*WH15: This is the No. 14 vase in the glossy finish. Photo courtesy of Glasstiques.*

*WH16: Notice the difference in color between the No. 14 vase in the previous photo, above left, and the one in this photo, right. As with any hand made glass, color variations are to be expected. Shown on the left is the No. 11 vase in the matte finish. Photo by Bill Pitt, courtesy of Brookside Antiques.*

*WH17: The No. 21 vase stands 15-3/4" tall.*

**WH18**: *The claret jug, No. 322 in the Hobbs catalogs.*

**WH19A**: *The pontil mark on one of the overfired claret jugs, shown below.*

**WH19**: *A pair of claret jugs which have been overfired during striking, a process in which the top of the item is reheated to achieve the color shading. Photo by Bill Pitt, courtesy of Brookside Antiques.*

*WH20*: *The No. 3 water bottle is scarce.*

*WH22*: *The No. 321 tankard is sometimes called the "stove pipe tankard" because of its height.*

*WH21*: *The pelican jug, which is No. 324 in the catalog, is one of Hobbs' most well-known shapes.*

**WH23**: *The 91-7 tankard is shorter and wider than the stove pipe tankard. Photo by Bill Pitt, courtesy of Brookside Antiques.*

**WH24**: *The 91-7 tankard in matte.*

**WH25**: *The 319 jugs come in five sizes, designated from 319/No. 5 to 319/No. 0. (There is no 319/No. 3) Shown here are the No. 5 and No. 4 in matte.*

*WH28: The ball cruet is the rarest of the cruet shapes and does not appear in the Hobbs catalogs. Photo by Bill Pitt, courtesy of Brookside Antiques.*

*WH27A: This shape is unusual without a handle. It appears to be the same as the No. 319 jug. Photo courtesy of Glasstiques.*

*WH27B: Same as above, only in glossy finish.*

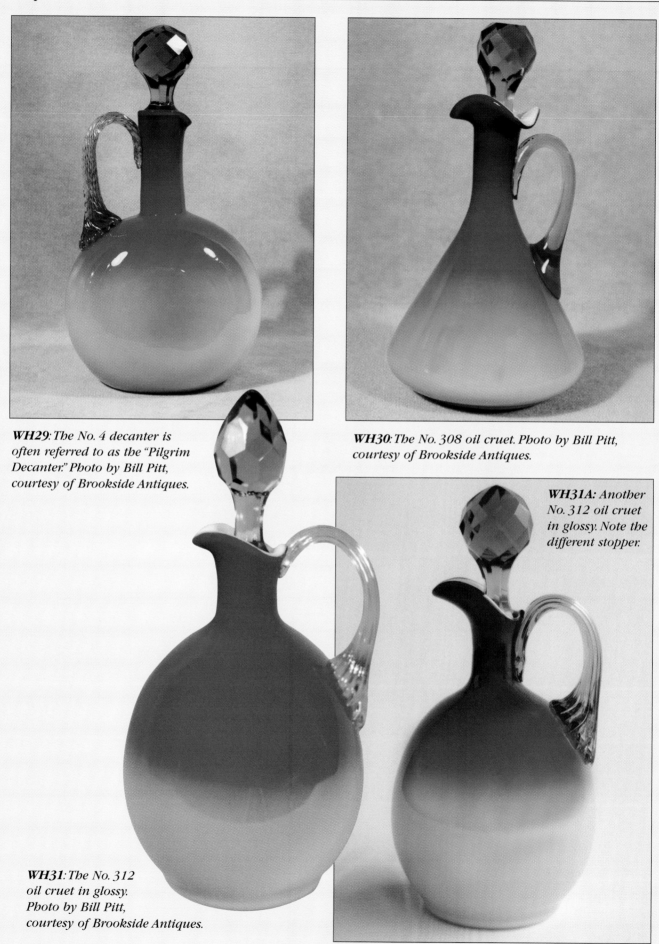

**WH29**: *The No. 4 decanter is often referred to as the "Pilgrim Decanter." Photo by Bill Pitt, courtesy of Brookside Antiques.*

**WH30**: *The No. 308 oil cruet. Photo by Bill Pitt, courtesy of Brookside Antiques.*

**WH31A**: *Another No. 312 oil cruet in glossy. Note the different stopper.*

**WH31**: *The No. 312 oil cruet in glossy. Photo by Bill Pitt, courtesy of Brookside Antiques.*

**WH32**: *This is the No. 1 spooner, which is smaller than the No. 314.*

**WH35**: *The No. 1 butter is a shallow bowl standing only 1-5/8" high x 4" wide.*

**WH33 & WH34**: *The No. 1 creamer, top, and the No. 1 sugar. Photos by Bill Pitt, courtesy of Brookside Antiques.*

*WH36: The No. 1 creamer and No. 1 sugar in a silver holder.*

*WH37: The No. 2 finger bowl. Photo courtesy of Glasstiques.*

*WH39: These vases come in five different sizes, designated as No. 0 through No. 5, but there's no No. 3. Photo by Bill Pitt, courtesy of Brookside Antiques.*

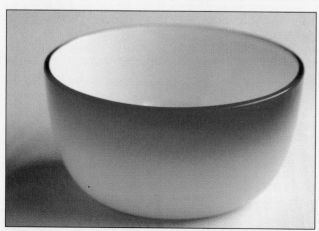

*WH42: The No. 93 finger bowl.*

*WH40: Same piece as above in glossy finish.*

**WH44**: The items shown in this Hartford Silver Plate Co. holder are the same items that came boxed as No. 226 salt, pepper and mustard.

**WH45**: The No. 226 mustard pot without the rest of the No. 226 set.

**WH43**: This is the No. 97 molasses can.

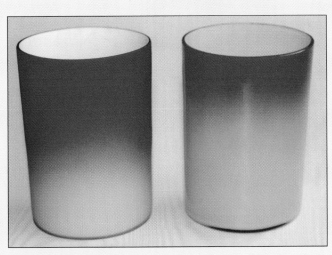

**WH47**: Another glossy tumbler. Compare the shadings on all three tumblers. Photo by Bill Pitt, courtesy of Brookside Antiques.

**WH46**: The tumbler is designated as No. 236, shown here in both glossy and matte.

**WH48**: *The No. 314 celery vase and No. 314 spooner are basically the same except for size.*

**WH49**: *What looks like a punch cup is designated in the catalog as No. 507 custard.*

**WH50A & WH50B**: *Two different sugar sifters, illustrating the variations in color. It's interesting that this shape was not given a numeric designation in the catalog.*

**WH51**:*Whimsies such as fruit don't appear in the catalogs either. Photo by Bill Pitt, courtesy of Brookside Antiques.*

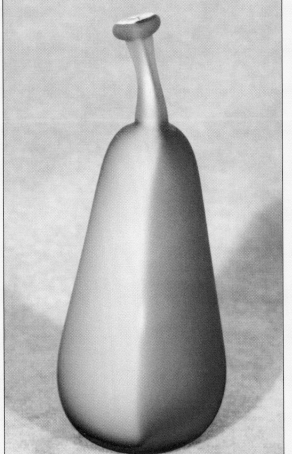

**WH52**:*A bi-colored pear. Note the white casing, visible at the top of the stem. Photo by Bill Pitt, courtesy of Brookside Antiques.*

**WH53**:*An apple showing the same coloration as the pear shown to the left. Photo by Bill Pitt, courtesy of Brookside Antiques.*

*Fac-simile Morgan ($18000) Vase and Stand*

**WH54**: *Shown here are the reprints of the original catalog pages from Hobbs, showing Peach Blow items. Note that this book does not include photos of the No. 321 tumbler, the No. 233 tumbler (with handle), the No. 247 champ tumbler, the No. 247 whiskey taster, the No. 8 vase or the No. 1 finger bowl. Catalog pages shown courtesy of Frank M. Fenton and Antique Publications.*

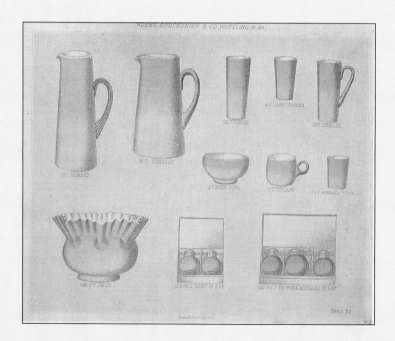

*Page from the Hobbs, Brockunier & Co. Catalog depicting (top row, L-R) No. 321 Tankard, No. 917 Tankard, No. 321 Tumbler, No. 247 Champ Tumbler, No. 322 Tumbler; (middle row, L-R) No. 2 Finger Bowl, No. 507 Custard, No. 247 Whiskey Tumbler; (bottom row, L-R) 4-in. 1715 Shade, No. 226 Salt & Pepper in box, No. 226 Salt, Pepper & Mustard in box.*

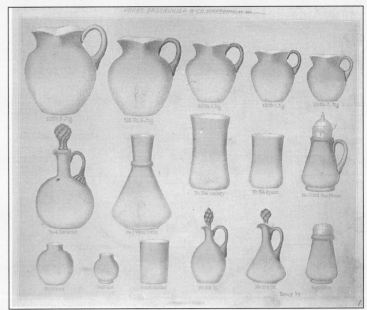

*Page from the Hobbs, Brockunier & Co. Catalog depicting (top row, L-R) 319 No. 5 Jug, 319 No. 4 Jug, 319 No. 2 Jug, 319 No. 1 Jug, 319 No. 0 Jug; (middle row, L-R) No. 4 Decanter, No. 3 Water Bottle, No. 314 Celery, No. 314 Spoon, No. 97 Mol. Gan Plated; (bottom row, L-R) No. 13 Vase, No. 9 Vase, No. 236 Tumbler, No. 312 Oil, No. 308 Oil, Sugar Sifter.*

*Page from Hobbs, Brockunier & Co. Catalog depicting (top row, L-R) No. 5 Vase, No. 4 Vase, No. 3 Vase, No. 2 Vase, No. 1 Vase, No. 0 Vase; (middle row, L-R) No. 6 Vase, No. 7 Vase, No. 7 Vase, No. 8 Vase, No. 322 Claret Jug, No. 11 Vase, No. 12 Vase; (bottom row, L-R) No. 1 Spoon, No. 1 Cream, No. 1 Sugar, No. 1 Butter, No. 93 Finger Bowl, No. 1 Finger Bowl.*

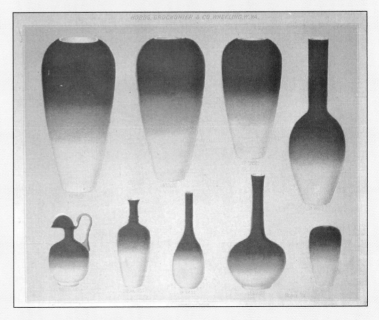

*Page from Hobbs, Brockunier & Co. Catalog depicting (top row, L-R) No. 19 Vase, No. 18 Vase, No. 17 Vase, No. 21 Vase; (bottom row, L-R) 324 Pelican Jug, 38 Vase, 14 Vase, 13 Vase, 23 Vase.*

**MW1:** *Frederick Shirley made this decoration famous when he sent several pieces of Burmese with this decoration to Queen Victoria of England. The design has since come to be known as the Queen's pattern. Here, it appears on peachblow, in a shape that vintage factory photographs of Burmese blanks are designated as number 146.*

# Mt. Washington Peachblow

It's unclear just how long Mt. Washington's line of peach-blow had been in the works before it appeared on the market. Patent number 332,294 for Mt. Washington's Burmese glass, issued Dec. 15, 1885, alludes to what we now know as peachblow.

Frederick S. Shirley, who acquired the Burmese patent for Mt. Washington, provides the formula for Burmese, which shades from rose pink to sulphur yellow, in the patent papers. This coloring comes from uranium oxide and prepared gold used as colorants. Patent papers go on to say that other elements could be substituted for the uranium oxide to alter the shading of the glass. Shirley does not describe the Mt. Washington peachblow coloration—a rose pink to pale blue—however. He states merely that carbonate of copper or oxide of chrome would create green to pale blue shading, chrome oxide and litharge would produce a shade of yellowish green shading into maroon or purple. Certainly the potential is there, and Shirley comes outright and states that he wants the patent to cover various chemical substitutions for different shaded effects. But the exact formula for Mt. Washington peachblow is not there, despite what has been reported elsewhere.

Mt. Washington peachblow was marked with paper labels and sold under the name "Peach Blow" or "Peach Skin." Other scholars have reported that when Mt. Washington obtained its patent for Burmese in December 1885, that it also acquired a trademark for the names "Peach Blow" and "Peach Skin." However we were unable to find a copy of the trademark at the US Patent and Trademark Depository in Philadelphia. Notes at Corning indicate the right to the word "peach" was granted to Mt. Washington through the Trade Mark Division of the US Patent Office and issued July 20, 1886, (#13,523) and that the name had been used since July 1, 1885.

The patent for Burmese does use the term "peach-skin," but not in reference to glassware of any particular color. Instead it seems to refer to shaded glassware of any color with a matte finish. The second to last paragraph of the patent says, "As a new manufacture, an article of glassware having one portion of a given color or tint shading into another color or tint, and having a roughened or lusterless surface, similar to a peach-skin, substantially as shown and described." Perhaps this is what other scholars have been referring to when they say Mt. Washington patented the term "Peach Skin" at the same time as Burmese.

No matter how the name came about, paper labels in

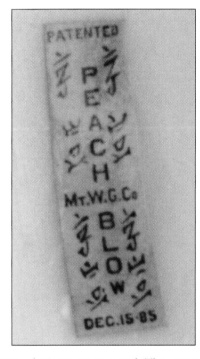

*MW2: The gourd vase with the Queen's design decoration even has its original rectangular paper label.*

two designs were used. The round label reads "Peach Skin" and the rectangular one says "Peach Blow." Interestingly, the rectangular label says "Patented Dec. 15, 85" which refers to the date of the patent for Burmese! Illustrations of the tags that we have seen have not included the patent date. However, we have seen two of these rectangular labels in person and both of these have the December 1885 date. This would seem to back up the story that Mt. Washington received a trademark for the name at the same time as it received the patent for Burmese. Maybe the variant that became Mt. Washington peachblow was produced before the Morgan sale. Or maybe the firm decided to add the December 1885 date to the labels because Shirley believed the Burmese patent would also cover this glass. Since we've not seen a round Peach Skin label, we don't know if it differs from illustrations we've seen.

Both labels incorporated Chinese characters, which would seem to indicate that the glassware was intended to imitate the porcelain. These characters are not the same ones used on the K'ang Hsi mark found on the Morgan vase, however.

Mt. Washington peachblow was not a commercial success and it literally sat on the shelves in the factory and in showrooms. It was out of production by 1888, and is the rarest form of peachblow today.

## Mt. Washington Peachblow Identification Card

**Proper Name:** "Peach Blow" or "Peach Skin."
**Manufacturer:** Mt. Washington Glass Co., New Bedford, MA.
**Date of Production:** 1886-1888.
**Color:** Shades from dusty rose to delicate blue gray.
**Casing:** None.
**Finish:** Both matte and glossy.
**Decorations:** Many of the same enamel designs found on Burmese.
**Special Characteristics:** The pontil mark is always concave and circular. Beware of pieces that do not exhibit this characteristic.

*MW3:A grouping of No. 146 gourd vases showing the shape both undecorated and decorated with different designs. These vases come in two sizes, an 8" version and a 12" version. Shown here are the larger ones.*

*MW4:The back of the vase on the left, shown in the previous photo. Photo by Bill Pitt, courtesy of Brookside Antiques.*

*MW5: This vase, designated as No. 148, is a little bit more slender than the 146. It has a lovely rose decoration with gold leaves. Photo by Bill Pitt, courtesy of Brookside Antiques.*

***MW6**: The double gourd vase was designated as No. 147 on vintage factory photos made available by Pairpoint in the 1950s. It stands about 7" tall. The decoration on the one on the right is called Prunus.*

**MW8:** *This is a lovely footed bowl with a lobed top.*

**MW7:**
*This corset vase stands 12-1/2" tall.*

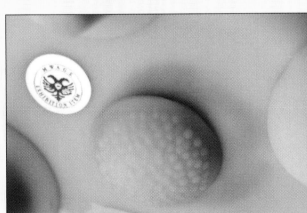

**MW8A:** *The prunt on the bottom of the footed bowl.*

**MW9:** *This footed bowl is a variation of the one above. Photo by Bill Pitt, courtesy of Brookside Antiques.*

*MW10:A Mt. Washington peach-blow pouch vase. It stands about 5" tall.*

*MW11: This hat-shaped ruffled bowl is about the same size as the pouch vase.*

*MW12: Mt. Washington peach-blow with applied peachblow decorations are extremely rare. This piece is a little bit smaller than the pouch vase and ruffled bowl. It appears to be No. 104 in the factory photograph, but it's difficult to be sure since the photo shows the shape only from the top.*

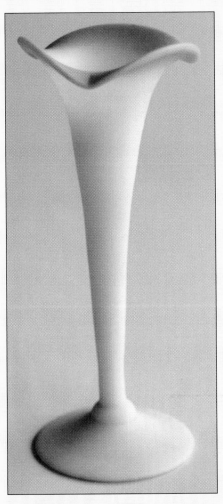

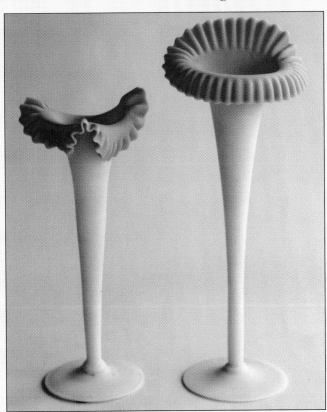

**MW13**:
A Mt. Washington
peachblow lily
vase.

**MW15**: The frilly lily, left, is the only one of its kind
known and is shown in George C. Avila's book, The
Pairpoint Glass Story. Seen more often is the crimped
jack-in-the-pulpit.

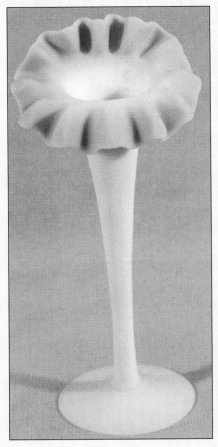

**MW16**: A smaller
jack-in-the-pulpit
with a less tightly
crimped rim. Photo
by Bill Pitt, courtesy
of Brookside
Antiques.

**MW17**: The
small jack-in-
the-pulpit, dec-
orated.

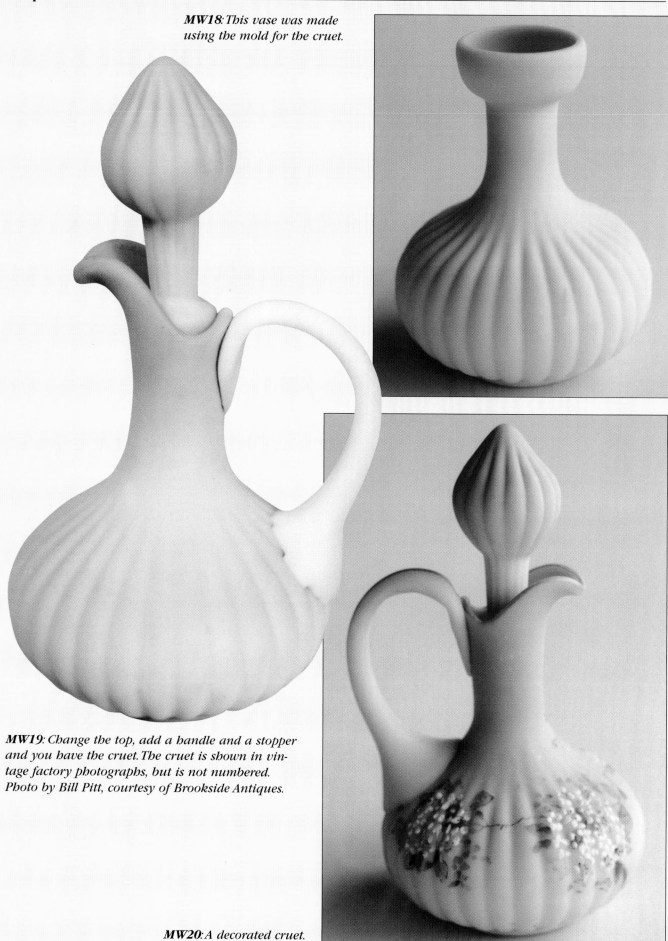

*MW18*: This vase was made using the mold for the cruet.

*MW19*: Change the top, add a handle and a stopper and you have the cruet. The cruet is shown in vintage factory photographs, but is not numbered. Photo by Bill Pitt, courtesy of Brookside Antiques.

*MW20*: A decorated cruet.

*MW21*: The oil bottle, decorated.

*MW22*: Ribbed salt shaker.

*MW23*: A lovely creamer and sugar set.

*MW25: Another sugar bowl, this one in a simple bowl shape, decorated with daisies. Photo courtesy of Glasstiques.*

*MW24: The wishbone sugar bowl is seldom found with this berry decoration.*

*MW27: A petticoat creamer with a tightly ruffled top.*

*MW26: Another style creamer.*

*MW28: This is the bulbous pitcher illustrated in the patent papers. It's rare in glossy. Photo by Bill Pitt, courtesy of Brookside Antiques.*

*MW29: The same pitcher, only in a matte finish and decorated.*

*MW30: Ruffled finger bowl.*

*MW31: A Mt. Washington peachblow tankard, left, and a bulbous pitcher.*

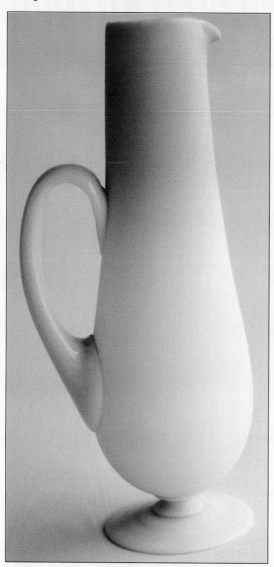

MW33: A decorated finger bowl, or shallow rose bowl, depending on how you see it.

MW32: A rare pedestal pitcher.

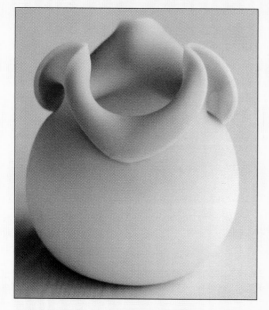

MW35: A tricornered bowl.

MW34: Another shape, also known as a rose bowl, with outward turned crimps.

**MW36:** *A pickle castor insert is quite rare in hobnail peachblow. Photo by Bill Pitt, courtesy of Brookside Antiques.*

**MW38:** *The rare hobnail design made into a cream pitcher.*

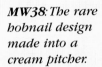

**MW39:** *A decorated square top toothpick holder.*

**MW37:** *The complete pickle castor, in Meridien silver.*

**MW40**: *A bulbous square top toothpick holder, shown alongside a tricorner toothpick holder.*

**MW41**: *A demitasse cup and saucer set in Mt. Washington peachblow. The old factory photo gave this shape the No. 139.*

**MW42**: *A lovely small decorated ruffled plate.*

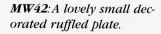

**MW43**: *The Mt. Washington peachblow tumbler and smaller whiskey taster are shown next to each other to illustrate the relative sizes. The whiskey taster stands 2-3/4˝ tall.*

**MW44**: Mt. Washington peachblow is a single layer, homogenous heat-sensitive glass. It gets its pink to blue-gray shading from striking, in which the glassmaker reheats a portion of the item. The reheating causes a chemical reaction which leads to the pink shading. When the glassmaker does not reheat a portion of the glass, the result is undeveloped peachblow. This ostrich egg perfume is undeveloped. It's decorated, so it was obviously intended to leave the factory without the pink shading.

**MW46**: Another example of an undeveloped peachblow salt.

**MW45**: Undeveloped peachblow salt shakers. Some people refer to undeveloped glass as "unfired." It means the same thing.

**MW47**: An undeveloped peachblow egg sugar shaker. Photo by Bill Pitt, courtesy of Brookside Antiques.

**MW49**: An undeveloped peachblow tomato salt shaker. Photo by Bill Pitt, courtesy of Brookside Antiques.

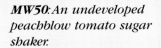

**MW50**: An undeveloped peachblow tomato sugar shaker.

**MW48**: An undeveloped peachblow egg sugar shaker. Photo by Bill Pitt, courtesy of Brookside Antiques.

*MW51: This full page ad, which mentions Peach Blow, appeared in a book titled* New Bedford, Massachusetts: Its History, Industries, Institutions and Attractions, *published in 1889 by the New Bedford Board of Trade.*

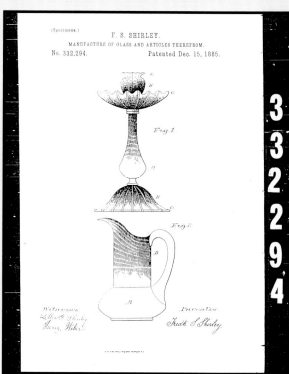

# UNITED STATES PATENT OFFICE.

--------------------

### FREDERICK STACEY SHIRLEY, OF NEW BEDFORD, MASS.

### MANUFACTURE OF GLASS AND ARTICLES THEREFROM.

----------

SPECIFICATION forming part of Letters Patent No. 332,294, dated December 15, 1885.

Application filed September 30, 1885. Serial No. 178,627. ( Specimens.)

----------

*To all whom it may concern:*

Be it known that I, Frederick S. Shirley, a citizen of the United States, residing at New Bedford, in the county of Bristol and [5] State of Massachusetts, have invented certain new and useful Improvements in the Manufacture of Glass and Articles Therefrom, of which the following is a specification, reference being had to the accompanying draw-[10]ings.

My invention and discovery consist, first, in a new mixture for glass, whereby I produce a new translucent glass, which, when formed into articles, shows entirely new and beauti-[15]ful effects; secondly, in new articles of manufacture from such glass; thirdly, in applying certain finishes to same, as more fully described hereinafter.

Figures 1 and 2 of the accompanying draw-[20]ings illustrate the articles.

A A show the original yellow or body color; B B B, the developed color. c c c show the points where reheating has reproduced the original body color.

[25] To carry out my invention I take one of the regular glass mixtures technically known as "lead" or "flint" glass consisting, say, of one hundred (100) pounds avoirdupois white sand, thirty-six (36) pounds refined lead oxide, [30] twenty-five (25) pounds of pearl ashes, five (5) pounds bicarbonate of soda, seven (7) pounds of niter. I make this translucent in any usual way, say, by adding six (6) pounds of fluor-spar and five (5) pounds of feldspar. [35] This batch produces a well-known mixture for translucent or opal glass, and my new mixture consists in a batch of this sort, to which both gold and uranium, or its described equivalents, are added, whereby a new glass [40] is produced, as more fully described below. To a batch such as above described I usually use two pounds avoirdupois of oxide of uranium and one and one half pennyweights of prepared gold, the whole to be thoroughly [45] mixed and melted in the usual manner known to the art. The proportions above mentioned may be varied, if desired, or equivalents substituted without departing from the spirit of my invention and discovery, which is the [50] combination of the oxide of uranium with pre-

pared gold, added to glass mixtures containing alumina, or its equivalent, when compounded, so as to form a translucent glass—for example, the fluor-spar and feldspar (both of which con-[55]tain alumina) may be omitted and cryolite and kaolin (which also contain alumina) substituted in equivalent proportions, care being taken to prevent the body being made too dense.

[60] Articles of glassware when made from this melted mixture will have a beautiful sulphur-yellow color throughout when first formed, but in finishing same in the usual manner in which such articles are made the metal or [65] material will develop a delicate pink shade on the portions last finished, this color shading into the original yellow body color. Should it be desired, the workman by reheating the edges to a melting point, can restore [70] the original yellow color on the part so reheated, thus producing varied effects of color shadings not previously obtainable.

My invention is the specific combination of a distinctive coloring agent—such as oxide of [75] uranium with prepared gold—and adding same to glass mixtures, which form a translucent glass body and contain alumina, or its equivalents, this last named material having a special effect on mixtures containing gold , con-[80]trolling the sensitive action of its coloring property in a marked degree. One peculiarity of my mixture, when melted, is that where the color is once developed on the article it is not sensitive to change from subsequent [85] reheatings, unless the heat is carried to such a high degree as to partially melt the glass, and another peculiarity is that the pink or developed color by such increased heat can be reduced, and the part so reheated to its origi-[90]nal yellow color, the workman taking care to keep the article in form by using his tools in the usual manner. The tint of yellow may be varied materially from a very pale primrose with a slight greenish tint to a deep sul-[95]phur yellow by increasing or diminishing the uranic oxide, and the pink or developed color may be varied in like manner from a pale salmon color to a deep rose by adding to or decreasing the proportion of gold; but, if the [100] latter is increased too much, the shades of color

will not be so delicate, and it will prevent the reaction of the developed color to its original body color. Carbonate of copper or oxide of chrome, combined with litharge, may be used [5] in lieu of the oxide of uranium with the prepared gold, and the above described translucent glass mixture and beautiful translucent glassware of other colors shading into each [10] other can be produced, and combination of other oxides with uranium and gold would give still other varieties of color, the first-named carbonate of copper producing ware of delicate greens to pale blue, (shade of color being dependent on the quantity used,) bodies [15] shading purple and rose color, that is developed in the finishing. The chrome oxide and litharge produce a shade of yellowish green, shading into a maroon or purple. When the mixture is melted in the pot, the workman [20] will gather sufficient metal on his blow-iron to form the article desired, and proceeds in identically the same manner well known to the art and as if making the same-shaped article from ordinary flint-glass, and without any care or [25] effort on his part the shaded effects described will be produced, and the article, when finished, will be annealed in the usual manner. I also produce a new and beautiful effect on this ware by removing the skin or glazing [30] from the surface of the article, either entirely or in parts only of the same, by abrading same with a sand-blast or immersing the articles in a bath suitable for that purpose. When desirable to retain the glaze on any portion, such [35] parts are to be protected by suitable cover or shield, or covered with wax or varnish, and the articles of this glass can be further ornamented by enamel colors, its resistance to heat without change of color rendering it specially [40] adaptable for this purpose, as enamel colors require a high heat to flux them. When carbonate of copper is used, the best proportion is nine ounces; for chrome and litharge, two ounces green oxide of chrome and ten pounds [45] of litharge well mixed with same, and it will also need an increase in amount of gold. The effects can be varied, as will be understood, by using a mixture of these coloring agents.

I am well aware of the so-called "opalescent [50] mixtures" that change in the working, and which contain bone ash and also tin, in combination with arsenic, and that the same have been combined with coloring oxides to produce white, greens, and blues. Most of these [55] have a flinty appearance with opalescent tints and when reheated develop shaded colors from the body-color to a white, the developed color being more or less opaque. These all

turn in the working by cooling and reheating the article, and are all well known to the art [60] for many years. I do not claim these; nor do I include manganese, which is frequently used as a corrector in all glass mixtures, in the term "distinctive coloring-oxides" for although, if used in excess, it would give a body-[65]color it would not be suitable for practical use with gold, and is not the equivalent, practically, of uranium, copper, or chrome and lead, and would not produce a color in contrast with that developed from the gold, and is well-known [70] for many years to have been used in combination with gold in coloring glass.

I am aware of the patents granted to Joseph Locke, dated July 24, 1883, and numbered 282,002, and of November 3, 1883, and num-[75]bered 288,582, and do not claim any of these inventions in this application.

Having described my invention, what I claim is—

1. A mixture for glass in which uranium [80] oxide or its described equivalent coloring agents and prepared gold are both added to glass batch containing alumina or its equivalents, for producing a translucent glass, substantially as described.

[85] 2. A mixture for producing colored translucent glassware, in which prepared gold and two or more distinctive coloring agents are used, in combination with alumina or its equivalents, substantially as specified.

[90] 3. As a new article of manufacture, an article of glassware of a translucent material having a body color due to a coloring agent such as is above described, and a developed color shading into the original body-color, substan-[95]tially as described.

4. As a new article of manufacture, an article of glassware formed from translucent material having a body color due to a coloring agent such as is above described, and a de-[100]veloped color shading into the original body-color and having a roughened or lusterless surface, substantially as described.

5. As a new manufacture, an article of glassware having one portion of a given color [105] or tint shading into another color or tint, and having a roughened or lusterless surface, similar to a peach-skin, substantially as shown and described .

In testimony whereof I affix my signature in [110] presence of two witnesses.

FREDK. STACEY SHIRLEY.

Witnesses:
Andrew Snow, Jr.,
Chas. F. Swift.

*MW53: The patent for Burmese alludes to peachblow, but doesn't come right out and give the formula. And, although it uses the term "peach-skin," the term clearly refers to a finish and not a type of glass.*

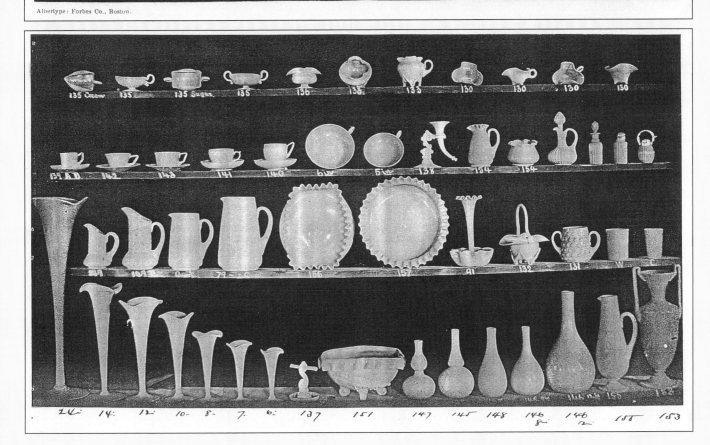

**BURMESE WARE.**

Albertype: Forbes Co., Boston.

**MW52A** *and* **MW52B**: *These vintage factory photographs illustrate the many shapes found in Burmese. Many of these shapes also exist in peachblow. These photos were originally published in Mt. Washington catalogs and then made available in 1958 by Pairpoint, who referred to them as "Burmese and Peachblow photos."*

*NE1: This decoration makes this stick vase rare. Photo by Bill Pitt, courtesy of Brookside Antiques.*

# New England Peachblow

It's been said that New England peachblow was the firm's answer to Mt. Washington Burmese. Certainly the public's positive response to shaded glassware such as Amberina and Burmese led to further experimentation on heat sensitive glass. So even if New England peachblow wasn't a direct response to Burmese, it was certainly indirect. The company filed its patent application on Oct. 3, 1886 and was granted patent number 337,170 on March 2, 1886, six days before the sale of the Morgan vase.

The formula for this glass was created by Joseph Locke and patented by Edward D. Libbey who avoided patent infringements for Burmese by stating that ingredients for opal glass and gold ruby glass should be mixed simultaneously in one batch. It was made at the Cambridge, Mass. factory only until the factory closed in 1888.

No clear cut information exists on just what this glass was called. Patent papers typically do not name the glass and the patent for this ware is no exception. We know for sure that this glass was marketed as Wild Rose. Albert C. Revi interviewed Joseph Locke's daughter and she said that her father referred to the line as "Peachblow." This would back up reports that the line was called "Peachblow" at the factory.

The November 4, 1886 issue of *Pottery and Glassware Reporter* includes an article which is more of a brief company history than a discussion of company products. It mentions Wild Rose, but refers to it once as "Peachblow" and a second time as "Peach Blow." The article says: "In recent years, four novelties have been brought out buy the New England Glass Works under Mr. Libbey's administration. We refer to the Amberina, Pomona, Peachblow and Agata grades of goods, the last mentioned being one of the most attractive novelties in glass goods ever offered to the public. We shall speak of this later on."

After discussing Amberina and Pomona, the article returns to Wild Rose. "The Peach Blow is another of the novelties of the New England Glass Works, and, as its name implies, is a sort of lucious ware in design among glass production, and maintains its position among the more recent popular and artistic wares."

As its name implies? Which name? Wild Rose, Peachblow or Peach Blow? Inconsistency in the use of names in original documents and trade journals seems to indicate that people back then weren't quite as concerned about it as we are today.

It's also ironic that the article refers to this line as a popular one when it was not particularly successful commer-

*NE2: New England made a variety of curio vases. Collection of Stu Horn.*

cially. Perhaps it was this lack of commercial success that inspired the company to invent Agata, which was essentially Wild Rose with a metallic staining applied so that it looks like oil floating on water. Trade journals do not refer to Agata as peachblow and it is still not thought of today as peachblow. It's worth mentioning that New England made a facsimile of the Morgan vase in Agata in about 1887. That's also interesting because the Agata version looks more like the actual porcelain vase than anything produced in any of the major types of peachblow. Perhaps the Morgan vase was copied in New England peachblow too, but so far no examples have surfaced.

It's also worth mentioning that on July 13, 1886, Locke obtained a patent for "Plated Wild Rose." This glassware consisted of a transparent layer of Wild Rose over an opal layer. This glass is considerably more scarce than regular Wild Rose. No known examples have been found.

---

**New England Peachblow Identification Card**

**Proper Name:** Wild Rose, but it was also called "Peachblow" or "Peach Blow" at the factory and in trade journals.

**Manufacturer:** New England Glass Works, Cambridge, MA.

**Date of Production:** 1886-1888.

**Color:** Shades from rose pink to white.

**Casing:** None.

**Finish:** Both matte and glossy. Glossy is less common.

**Decorations:** Enameled designs, gold tracery or gold trim, applied white handles or rigaree.

**Special Characteristics:** The pontil mark is usually concave and circular, but sometimes these pieces are found with rough pontils.

*NE3: This curio vase is similar to the one in NE2, but the base is thinner and the top is higher. Photo by Bill Pitt, courtesy of Brookside Antiques.*

*NE4: Another curio vase.*

*NE5: This curio vase has a band of applied rigaree around the center.*

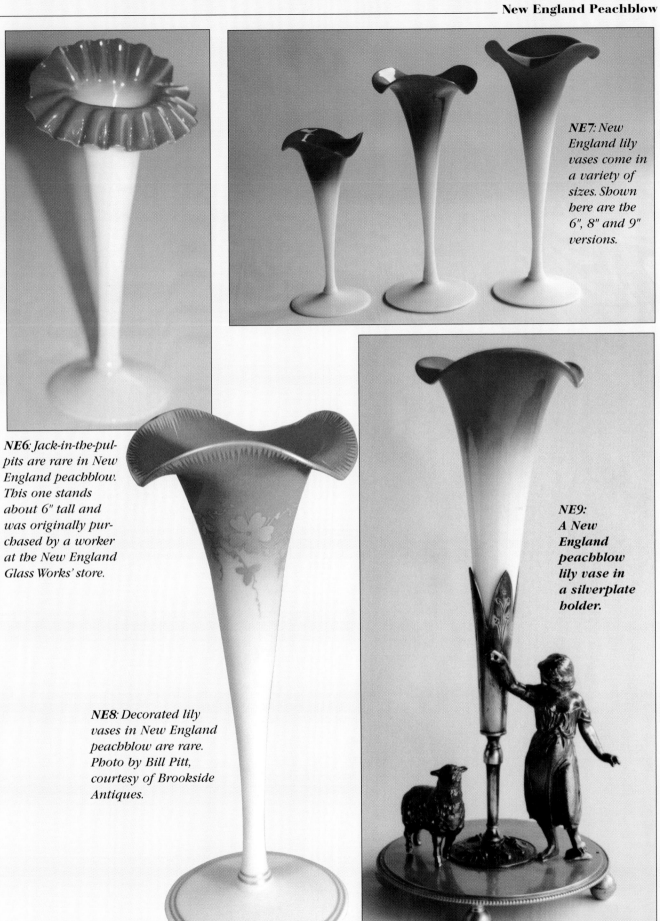

**NE7**: *New England lily vases come in a variety of sizes. Shown here are the 6", 8" and 9" versions.*

**NE6**: *Jack-in-the-pulpits are rare in New England peachblow. This one stands about 6" tall and was originally purchased by a worker at the New England Glass Works' store.*

**NE9: A New England peachblow lily vase in a silverplate holder.**

**NE8**: *Decorated lily vases in New England peachblow are rare. Photo by Bill Pitt, courtesy of Brookside Antiques.*

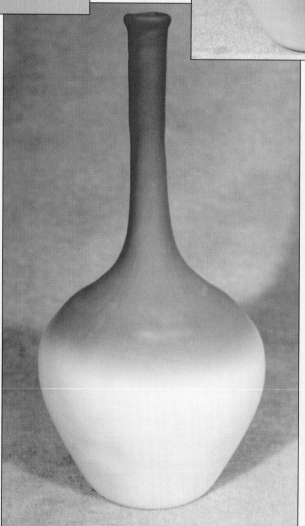

**NE10:** *Here's an unusual shape, best described as a cup vase. Photo courtesy of Glasstiques.*

**NE11** *and* **NE11A**: *These two bulbous stick vases illustrate the range of coloration to be found in the New England line. Photos by Bill Pitt, courtesy of Brookside Antiques.*

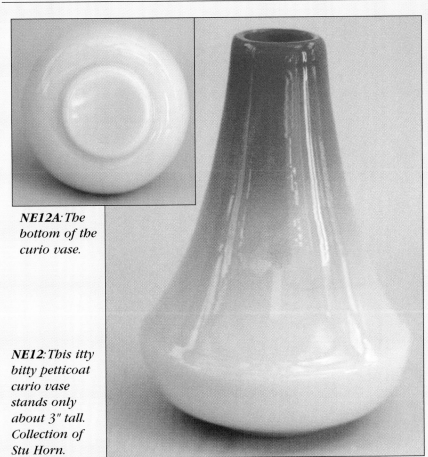

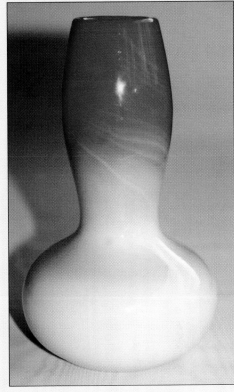

**NE12A:** *The bottom of the curio vase.*

**NE12:** *This itty bitty petticoat curio vase stands only about 3" tall. Collection of Stu Horn.*

**NE13:** *A New England peachblow gourd vase.*

**NE14:** *A decorated gourd vase and a pinched gourd vase.*

**NE15:** *The large size of this piece makes it interesting and desirable. Photo courtesy of Glasstiques.*

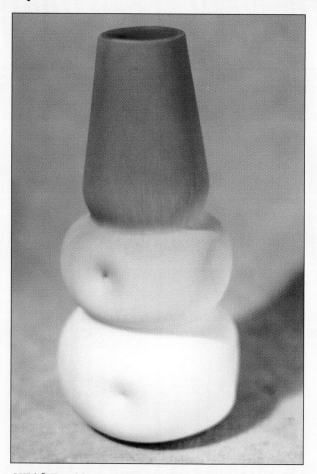

**NE16**: *Double gourd vase with pinched sides.*

**NE17**: *An interesting vase. Photo by Bill Pitt, courtesy of Brookside Antiques.*

**NE18A**: *Bulbous vase with flared top. Photo by Bill Pitt, courtesy of Brookside Antiques.*

**NE18B**: *The same piece, in a glossy finish. Photo courtesy of Glasstiques.*

*NE19: The enameled design makes this vase outstanding.*

*NE20: A bulbous bottom vase.*

*NE21: A pouch vase decorated with a spider in its web hoping to snare dinner.*

*NE22:  This vase is deceptively light.*

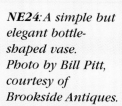

**NE23**: *This vase is similar to NE22.*

**NE24**: *A simple but elegant bottle-shaped vase. Photo by Bill Pitt, courtesy of Brookside Antiques.*

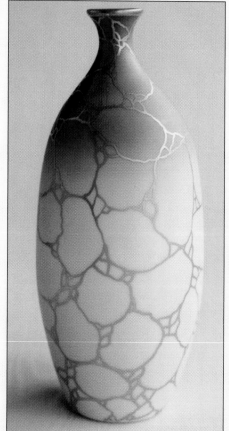

**NE25**: *The bottle vase takes on a whole new look with the tracery design.*

**NE26**: *This large vase is gorgeous with gold fern decoration. Photo by Bill Pitt, courtesy of Brookside Antiques.*

*NE28: Vase with a tightly ruffled top.*

*NE27: A vase with a ruffled tricorner rim. Photo by Bill Pitt, courtesy of Brookside Antiques.*

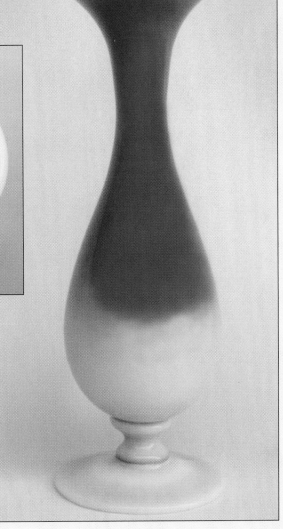

*NE30: The pontil is rough, which is unusual for New England peachblow, but it is authentic.*

*NE29: The bud vase is an unusual shape in New England peachblow.*

*NE32A: Celery, matte finish. Notice how the color change is more gradual on this piece than on the glossy one in the next photo. Photo by Bill Pitt, courtesy of Brookside Antiques.*

*NE31: This celery vase is unusual because it's pinched. Photo by Bill Pitt, courtesy of Brookside Antiques.*

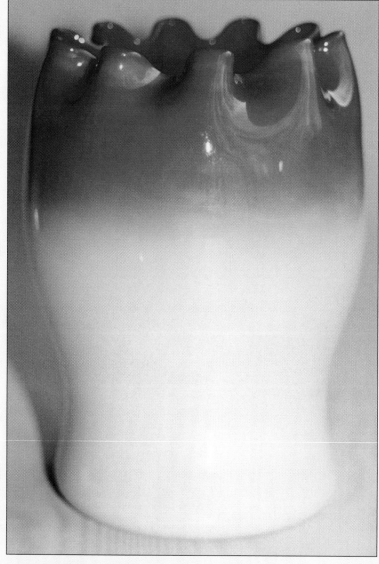

*NE32B: Celery, glossy finish.*

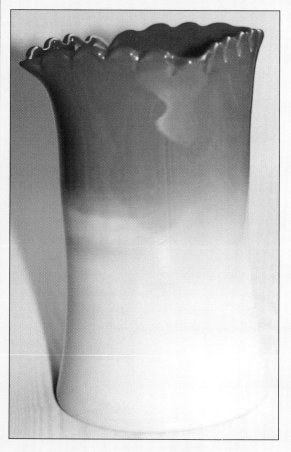

*NE33: The top flares out slightly on this celery vase.*

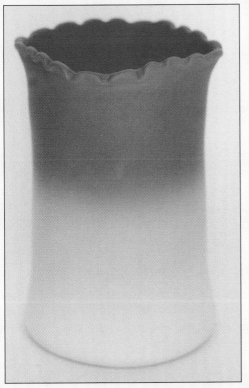

*NE34: Other than the top, it's the same shape as, only taller than, the spooner.*

*NE35: Leaf shaped one-handled nappy.*

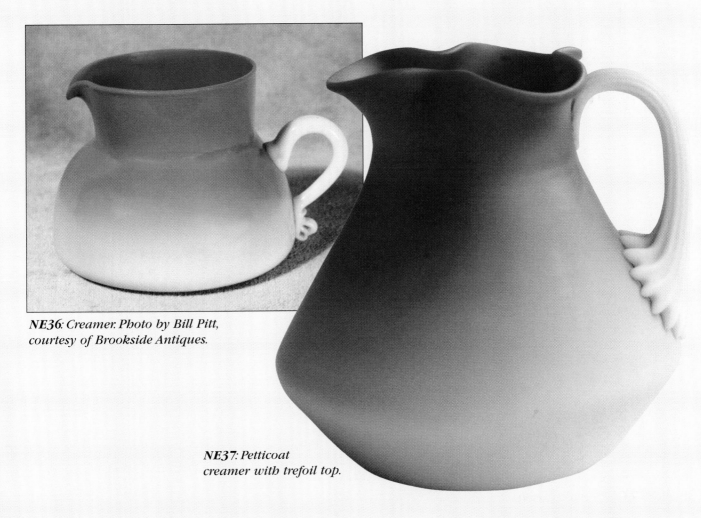

*NE36: Creamer. Photo by Bill Pitt, courtesy of Brookside Antiques.*

*NE37: Petticoat creamer with trefoil top.*

**NE38:** *It's unusual to find this piece without the handle.*

**NE39:** *This shape in a creamer and sugar set is unusual.*

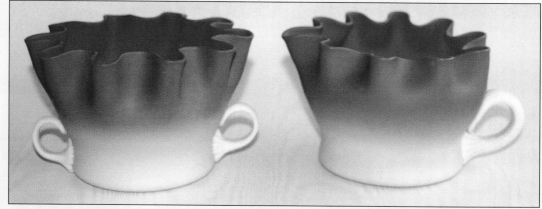

**NE40A:** *Cruet.*

**NE40B:** *Cruet. Photo by Bill Pitt, courtesy of Brookside Antiques.*

*NE41: Note the size difference between the glossy tankard and the matte milk pitcher.*

*NE41B: Another shot of a tankard. Photo by Bill Pitt, courtesy of Brookside Antiques.*

*NE42: The square top pitcher comes in both a 4-1/2" size and an 8-1/2" size.*

***NE43***: *Glass companies often used the same basic shape for more than one piece. This milk pitcher resembles the celery in NE32. Photo courtesy of Glasstiques.*

*NE44: Tricorner toothpick holder.*

*NE45A: Square top toothpick holder in silver-plate figural Kate Greenaway holder.*

*NE45B: The coloring on the toothpick in this holder is considerably different than the other. Photo by Bill Pitt, courtesy of Brookside Antiques.*

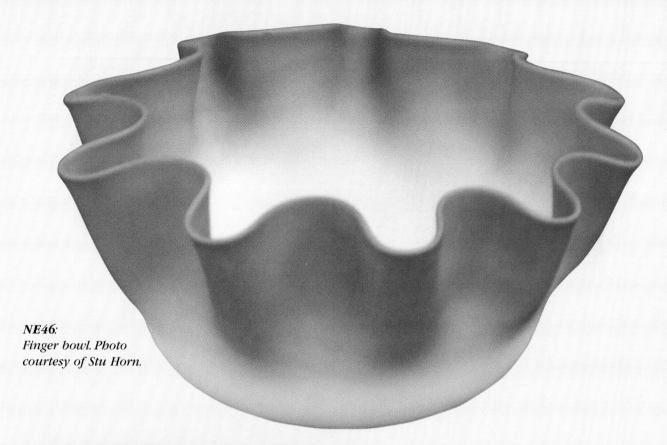

*NE46:*
*Finger bowl. Photo*
*courtesy of Stu Horn.*

*NE47: The finger bowl is hard to find with the matching underplate.*

*NE48: Ruffled finger or berry bowl in glossy finish.*

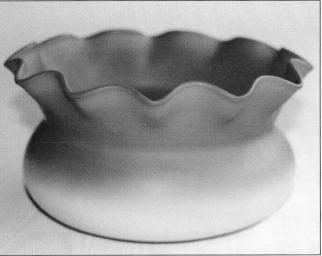

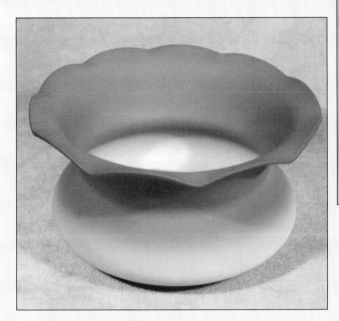

*NE50: The berry or ice cream bowl is larger than the finger or berry bowl.*

*NE49: Ruffled finger or berry bowl in matte finish. Photo by Bill Pitt, courtesy of Brookside Antiques.*

*NE51: This large bowl was probably intended to be a berry bowl.*

**NE52:** *A small finger bowl with a smooth rim, which could have also served as an ice cream bowl or berry bowl.*

**NE53:** *A salt shaker. Photo by Bill Pitt, courtesy of Brookside Antiques.*

**NE54:** *A pair of shakers in a frame marked "F.B. Rogers Silver Co., 1883 Taunton, Mass."*

*NE55: Punch cup, glossy finish.*

*NE57: A typical New England peach-blow pontil mark.*

*NE56: Punch cup, matte finish.*

**NE58:** *Two whiskey tasters. Smaller than tumblers, these are about the size of what today would be considered a small juice tumbler.*

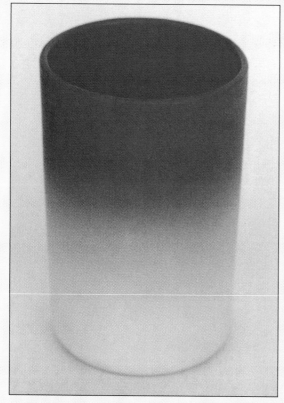

**NE59:** *Tumbler. Photo courtesy of Glasstiques.*

**NE60:** *This is the only known example of New England peachblow with a Pomona staining and a cut fern decoration.*

_**NE61:** New England peachblow was originally sold with small paper labels that look like this. These labels are seldom found today. Shown considerably larger than actual size._

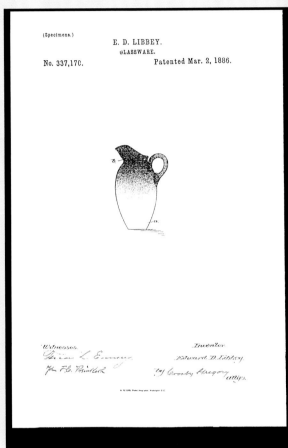

_**NE62:** The original patent for Wild Rose._

## UNITED STATES PATENT OFFICE.

------------------

### EDWARD D. LIBBEY, OF WINCHESTER, MASSACHUSETTS.

### GLASSWARE.

----------

SPECIFICATION forming part of Letters Patent No. 337,170, dated March 2, 1886.

Application filed October 3, 1885. Serial No. 178,873. ( Specimens. )

-----------

_To all whom it may concern:_

Be it known that I, Edward D. Libbey, of Winchester, county of Middlesex, and State of Massachusetts, have invented an Improve-
5 ment in Glassware, of which the following description, in connection with the accompanying drawing, is a specification, like letters on the drawing representing like parts.

This invention has for its object the pro-
10 duction of novel opaque glassware of attractive appearance.

My invention consists in glassware of homogeneous opaque material, opposite ends or different parts of the said article, although
15 homogeneous material, presenting different colors or shades of colors blended together.

The drawing represents an article of glassware embodying my invention.

In the practice of my invention I take an
20 ordinary opaque or opal glass mixture and add to it a quantity of glass mixture suitable for the production of what is known as "ruby-glass containing gold," the quantity of this last mixture being however variable, according to
25 the density of the color to be developed by reheating the glass after cooling.

The opaque glass mixture and the ruby glass mixture referred to are melted to form a homogeneous body, and by usual processes is
30 blown and shaped into an article of glassware of the shape which is desired to produce. The article, having been shaped and somewhat cooled, is then reheated at that end or part of it which is to have a darker color developed
35 upon it, the reheating being preferably at the "glory-hole." The end or part of the article so reheated will have developed upon it a color different from that due to the opaque or opal glass mixture if used alone, the developed

color being entirely different from what would 40 have been the color of the article had it not been partially reheated after being somewhat cooled.

In the drawing, _a_ represents the part of the article (shown as a pitcher,) which is of the 45 color due to the opaque glass mixture, the part _b_ being that developed by reheating the shaped article.

It is obvious that I may produce from the glass mixture referred to any desired article 50 of glassware , such as vases, jugs, &c.

An article produced from the glass mixture so far described would at the end _a_ be of a white color, due to the opaque or opal glass mixture employed, and the developed color 55 at _b_, due to the ruby glass mixture containing gold, would be a shade of red.

By methods and means familiar to all practical glass-makers the opaque glass mixture may be made to present various colors—as , for 60 instance, the addition of a little uranium to the mixture will produce an opaque glass of a yellow color, while copper or cobalt will produce a blue color. Other different metallic oxides will produce yet other colors. 65

I claim--

As an improved article of manufacture, glassware of homogeneous opaque material, portions of which present different colors or shades of color blended together, substan- 70 tially as described.

In testimony whereof I have signed my name to this specification in the presence of two subscribing witnesses.

EDWARD D. LIBBEY.

Witnesses:

G. W. GREGORY,

B. J. NOYES.

**WF5: A typical World's Fair peachblow rose bowl. Neither Mt. Washington nor Libbey made peachblow rose bowls with this crimp style. It appears this shape was created just for the World's Fair. Authors' collection.**

# CHAPTER 6

# World's Fair Peachblow

In 1893, Edward D. Libbey, acting on behalf of the Libbey Glass Co., obtained the exclusive right to set up a factory at the World's Columbian Exposition in Chicago. Fair goers could see glass being manufactured on site and could purchase pieces for souvenirs.

Libbey's factory included a single furnace with eight or ten pots and employed about 300 people, about half of whom were glassblowers. Because Libbey was the successor to the New England Glass Works, the peachblow items produced were made with the original New England formula. A number of other types of souvenir glass were produced, including a solid cornflower blue and a yellow that looks much like undeveloped Burmese. But these should not be confused with peachblow. Incorrect labels such as "blue peachblow" and "yellow peachblow" are sometimes found on glassware at shops and shows. But there is no such thing as either blue peachblow or yellow peachblow.

Sugars, creamers, pears, sock darners, rose bowls and jack-in-the pulpits were the most common shapes, but others are also found. Many of these items are found decorated with fancy scrollwork and the words "World's Fair 1893." The Smith Brothers of New Bedford, Mass., who once worked as decorators for Mt. Washington, are known to have done some of the decorating.

The Libbey factory proved to be a hit, so much so that workers could not keep up with demand. It is believed that the company commissioned Mt. Washington to produce some souvenir glass items and the peachblow items were made using the New England formula. Mt. Washington items tend to have pink or dark pink coloration at the top where Libbey items show a more deep rose or purplish red.

**WF1**: *Souvenir peachblow pears are probably the most commonly found World's Fair items. Be careful of reproductions. Photo courtesy of Louise Nadeau.*

So far, no paper trail proving Mt. Washington's involvement has turned up, but the existence of their shapes in this ware cannot be denied.

---

### World's Fair Peachblow Identification Card

**Proper Name:** Uncertain. Peach Blow or Peachblow is possible.
**Manufacturer:** Libbey Glass Co., Toledo, Ohio, and Mt. Washington, on site.
**Date of Production:** 1893.
**Color:** Rose pink to lighter pink to almost white.
**Casing:** None.
**Finish:** Both matte and glossy, though glossy is scarcer.
**Decorations:** Many pieces are undecorated, but some are also found decorated with "World's Fair 1893" in fancy gold scrolling. A few pieces will have other decorations.
**Special Characteristics:** World's Fair peachblow was intended to be cheap souvenir glass. As a result, it is lighter in weight than New England peachblow and the pontils are not polished.

*WF2: A decorated World's Fair peachblow pear.*

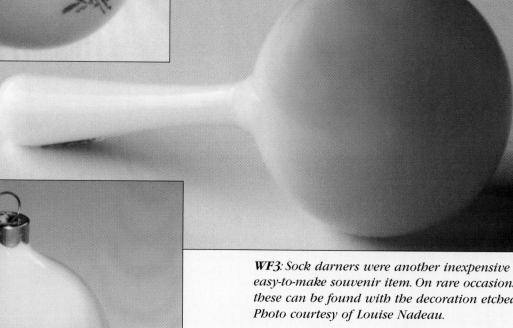

*WF3: Sock darners were another inexpensive easy-to-make souvenir item. On rare occasions, these can be found with the decoration etched. Photo courtesy of Louise Nadeau.*

*WF4: What do you do when the handle breaks off your sock darner? Make it into a Christmas ornament! That's what happened to this one. Christmas ornaments were not originally made in World's Fair peachblow.*

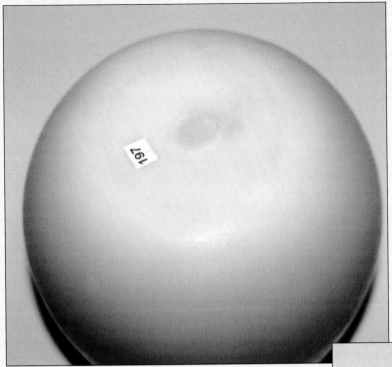

**WF6**: *The pontil is a dead giveaway that this piece is not New England peachblow, but a World's Fair piece.*

**WF7**: *A selection of World's Fair peachblow rose bowls, both undecorated and decorated. They're found in a variety of sizes.*
*Right Photo courtesy of Irmgard Schmidt.*
*Below Collection of Stu Horn.*

**WF8:** *A World's Fair peachblow rose bowl in the hard-to-find glossy finish. Collection of Stu Horn.*

**WF9A:** *World's Fair peachblow rose bowls with subtle ribbing in the glass are scarce. Note the decoration.*

**WF9B:** *Another ribbed World's Fair peachblow rose bowl, this one undecorated. Authors' collection.*

*Photo by
Bill Pitt,
courtesy
of
Brookside
Antiques.*

**WF10:** *Shown here are two World's Fair peachblow jack-in-the-pulpits. They come in three sizes and the coloration often varies.*

**WF11:** *A pair of ribbed World's Fair peachblow creamers. This petticoat style is harder to find than other creamer shapes.*

**WF12**: A decorated World's Fair peach-blow creamer. Decorations as nice as this are difficult to find. Photo by Bill Pitt, courtesy of Brookside Antiques.

**WF13**: This jack-in-the-pulpit is an unusual shape for World's Fair peach-blow. The etched decoration is unusual also.

**WF14**: A creamer and sugar decorated with the World's Fair 1893 logo.

*WF15*: *A rare egg-style World's Fair peachblow salt shaker. This is a distinctive Mt. Washington shape.*

*WF16*: *Another distinctive Mt. Washington shape is this rose bowl, shown here in World's Fair peachblow.*

*G1: Gundersen peachblow in a classic-shaped urn.*

# ❦ CHAPTER 7 ❦

# Gundersen Peachblow

Fully appreciating Gundersen peachblow and its place in glass history requires a brief history of the company.

Gundersen is actually a successor to Mt. Washington, which had been purchased on July 14, 1894 by the Pairpoint Corporation for $1 and other "valuable considerations." Mt. Washington and Pairpoint were located next to each other and shared many of the same shareholders and directors already.

For 35 years, the company did well. In the 1930s, however, Pairpoint was hit hard by Japanese competition. In November 1937, the glass and silver departments were closed and were sold in May 1938 to J.B. Kenner Inc., who resold them in June 1939. The buyer was a local group which included Robert Gundersen, a well-respected glassmaker who had been in charge of the division. The company name was then changed to the Gundersen Glass Works.

In 1952, upon Gundersen's death, the name of the company was changed to Gundersen-Pairpoint. In 1953, Robert Bryden joined the firm. He would eventually become the owner and move the glass works from New Bedford to East Wareham, MA.

It's been widely reported that Gundersen peachblow was made using the original Mt. Washington peachblow formula. This would make sense since Gundersen is a successor to Mt. Washington. However, a look at Gundersen peachblow should cause doubt. It shades from pink to white, not dusty-rose to blue-gray, the way Mt. Washington peachblow does. Since Mt. Washington apparently produced World's Fair peachblow items using the New England formula, Gundersen had that formula available when they reissued peachblow in the 1940s. This is apparently what they used, though for some reason the glass is heavier than New England or World's Fair peachblow.

Perhaps part of the reason for the confusion is a letter dated April 1, 1953 sent to dealers by the Gundersen Pairpoint Glass Works announcing the availability of peachblow. The letter states the glass is made from the original Mt. Washington formula, even though a visual inspection of the glass contradicts this.

"Pairpoint wishes to announce the limited availability of Peach Blow," the letter begins. "Turning back the years to 1885 when Peach Blow was first made at these works under the Mt. Washington name, our artisans, using the original formula, have succeeded in recapturing the delicate glass which has been a collector's item for many years. All are off-hand, free-hand Pairpoint craftsmanship made under the direction of the well-known Hjalmar Gulbranson, and are limited in design as shown. You are

*G2: Banjo vase.*

invited to contact us through our New England representatives, the H. L. Cobbett Associates, or to write or visit us directly here at the glass works."

The letter was signed by Gulbranson, even though it was Robert Bryden's name that was printed on it.

Although the company was named Gundersen-Pairpoint after Robert Gundersen's death in 1952, the glassware continues to be known to collectors as Gundersen Peachblow.

Gundersen peachblow was made until early 1957. The New Bedford plant closed in 1956 with the owners setting up shop in Wareham, MA. Some peachblow was made in Wareham, but not much. The Wareham plant closed in 1958.

**Gundersen Peachblow Identification Card**

**Proper Name:** Peach Blow or Peachblow (both spellings were used on company documents).

**Manufacturer:** Gundersen Glass Works, New Bedford, MA.

**Date of Production:** 1940s to 1957.

**Color:** Pink to white.

**Casing:** None.

**Finish:** Both matte and glossy.

**Decorations:** Some pieces will have applied white handles. No painted decorations.

**Special Characteristics:** Both rough and polished pontil marks are found. Don't confuse Gundersen with New England peachblow, which is the same color, but much thinner. Also, be skeptical of pieces tagged "Gundersen peachblow" when you don't know the seller. Many sellers think they have Gundersen peachblow when what they really have is 1960s Italian Burmese or 1960s Italian peachblow. (See Chapter 9.)

*G3: A pair of Gundersen peachblow cornucopias. These originally wholesaled for $4 apiece.*

*G4: Trumpet vase. Photo by Bill Pitt, courtesy of Brookside Antiques.*

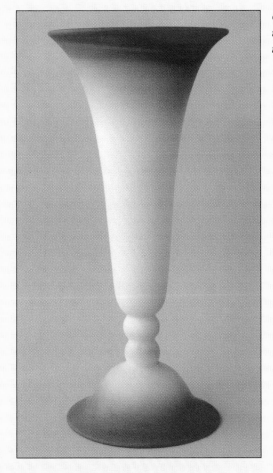

***G5***:*A rare trumpet vase with an unusual base.*

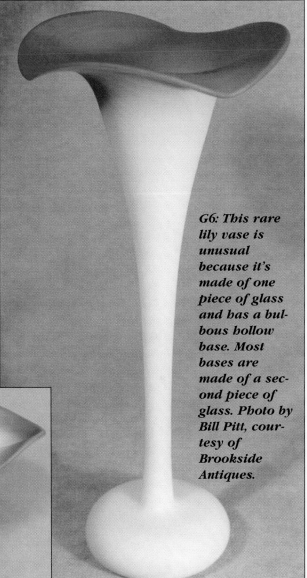

***G6: This rare lily vase is unusual because it's made of one piece of glass and has a bulbous hollow base. Most bases are made of a second piece of glass. Photo by Bill Pitt, courtesy of Brookside Antiques.***

***G7***:*Two Gundersen peachblow jack-in-the-pulpits. Photo by Bill Pitt, courtesy of Brookside Antiques.*

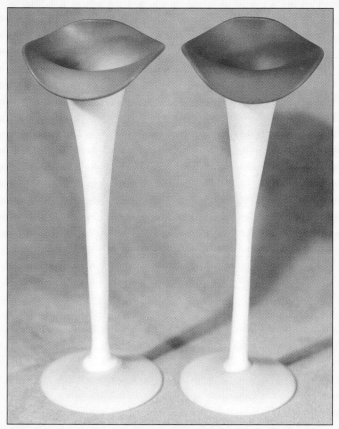

**G8:** *Another pair of jack-in-the-pulpit vases. Note the differences in color between this pair and those in the previous photo. Photo by Bill Pitt, courtesy of Brookside Antiques.*

**G10:** *This vase mimics a New England shape. A familiarity with the weight and feel of the glass is what is required to properly identify it. Photo by Bill Pitt, courtesy of Brookside Antiques.*

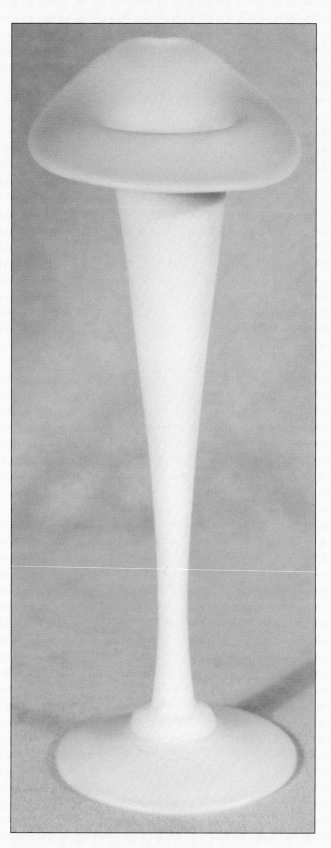

**G9:** *Another jack-in-the-pulpit with a different style trumpet and an unusually light color.*

*G11: A bud vase.*

*G12: A wide shoulder vase. Photo by Bill Pitt, courtesy of Brookside Antiques.*

*G13: A compote with a ruffled top. It was sold originally as either a nut dish or a bon-bon. It's hard to say for sure which, because no measurements are given for either of these in original documents. It would have wholesaled for either $4.50 or $5, depending on which it was. Photo by Bill Pitt, courtesy of Brookside Antiques.*

*G14: A compote with a smooth rim. Photo by Bill Pitt, courtesy of Brookside Antiques.*

*G15: This compote is unusual because of the blown hollow stem.*

*G16: This is a scarce and desirable swirl connector compote. It is designated as No. 3146 compote in an old Gundersen price list, and it wholesaled for $5. Photo by Bill Pitt, courtesy of Brookside Antiques.*

*G17: The "Morning Glory" console bowl was made with candlesticks to match (not shown).*

*G18: A Paul Revere bowl in the shape made famous in Paul Revere silver. Photo by Bill Pitt, courtesy of Brookside Antiques.*

*This sticker is on the handled decanter in the back left of the photo below. Even though the sticker says Pairpoint, and the company was Gundersen-Pairpoint, the glass is known as Gundersen peachblow.*

*G19: The relative sizes of handled decanters and cruets can be seen in this photo. The cruets are the two smaller pieces in the front. The Gundersen-Pairpoint Glass Works put Pairpoint stickers on some of their glass.*

*G20:* Another cruet like the one in the front, right, on the previous photo. Note how the stopper on this one is all white, however. Photo by Bill Pitt, courtesy of Brookside Antiques.

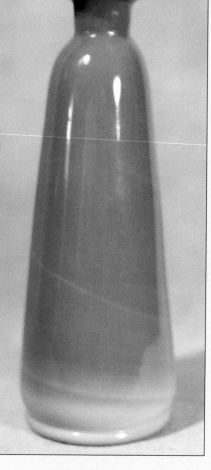

*G21:* A footed decanter without a handle. Photo by Bill Pitt, courtesy of Brookside Antiques.

*G22:* A perfume bottle. Photo by Bill Pitt, courtesy of Brookside Antiques.

**G23**: A perfume with an extremely rare floral stopper. Photo by Bill Pitt, courtesy of Brookside Antiques.

**G24:** An extremely rare perfume with a Charles Kaziun paperweight stopper made in the 1940s when Gundersen did paperweights. The flower inside the paperweight is also made of peachblow glass. Kaziun is the only Gundersen paperweight maker to have worked with peachblow glass and only a few of these are known to exist. Collection of Louis O. St. Aubin, Jr.

**G24A**: The stopper to the perfume, shown so the flower is visible.

*G25*: *Although the firm didn't announce the availability of peachblow until 1952, workers had been making a few items since the 1930s. This creamer was made by Anders Theon in the late 1930s for his own use.*

*G26: Two Gundersen creamers. The single straight handle on the one to the right is unusual.*

*G27*: *A ribbed creamer with a matching sugar. The sugar originally wholesaled for $3.50. Photo by Bill Pitt, courtesy of Brookside Antiques.*

**G28:** *Two creamers without the ribbed design in the glass, and a matching sugar.*

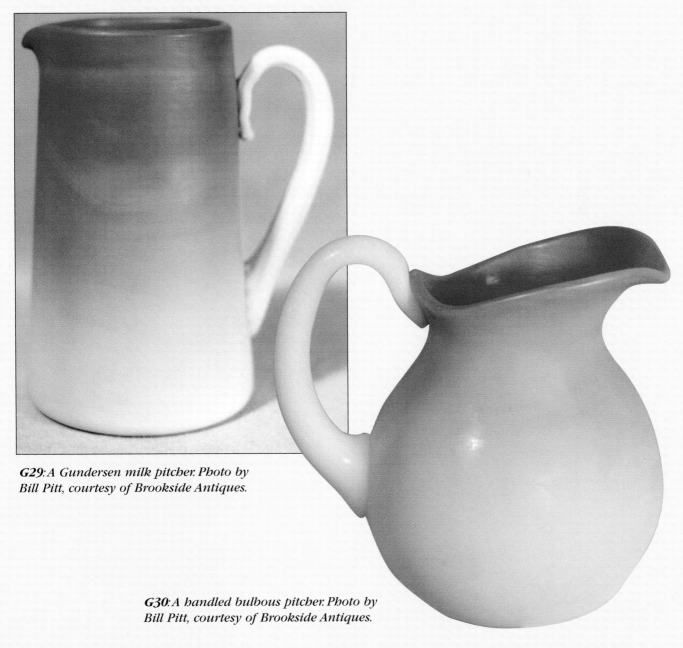

**G29:** *A Gundersen milk pitcher. Photo by Bill Pitt, courtesy of Brookside Antiques.*

**G30:** *A handled bulbous pitcher. Photo by Bill Pitt, courtesy of Brookside Antiques.*

*G31: Sherbet. Photo by Bill Pitt, courtesy of Brookside Antiques.*

*G32: This pair of goblets or chalices appear to have yellow feet. That's not trick photography. The feet are Burmese. Photo by Bill Pitt, courtesy of Brookside Antiques.*

*G33: Smaller than the goblet, this is the wine.*

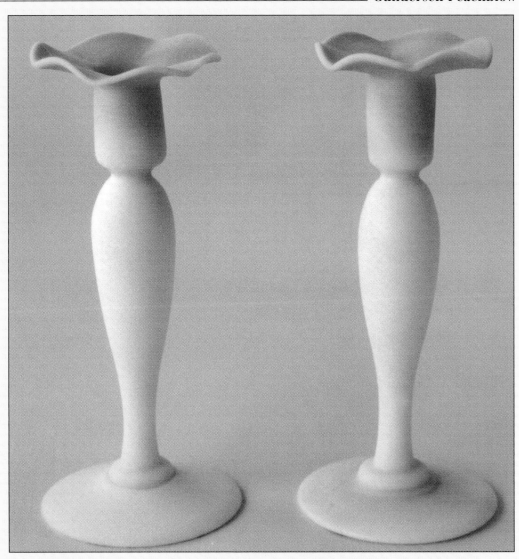

*G34:*
*These are the*
*8-1/2" crimped*
*candlesticks.*
*They wholesaled*
*for $4 apiece.*

*G35: These are Gundersen's waterfall candlesticks which are quite rare in peachblow.*

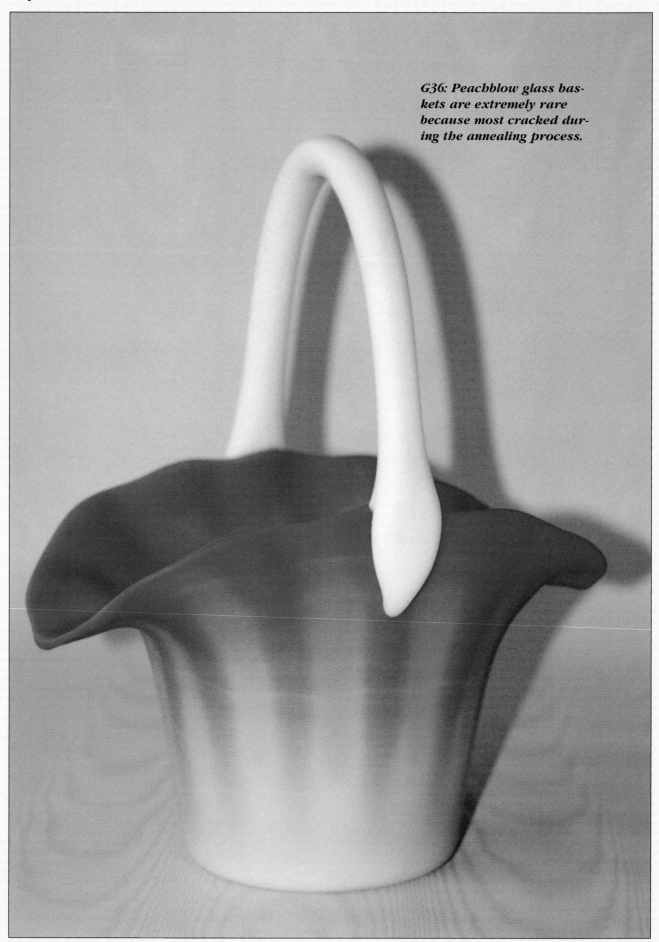

*G36: Peachblow glass bas-
kets are extremely rare
because most cracked dur-
ing the annealing process.*

*G37: A peachblow overlay cut to clear paperweight. Less than a half dozen of these are known to exist. They were experimental pieces made during the 1950s.*

*G38: Several sizes of plates were made in peachblow. This is the luncheon plate.*

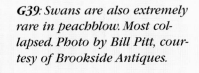

*G39: Swans are also extremely rare in peachblow. Most collapsed. Photo by Bill Pitt, courtesy of Brookside Antiques.*

*G40: A Gundersen peachblow cup and saucer. The cup wholesaled for $3.25 and the cup for $2.50.*

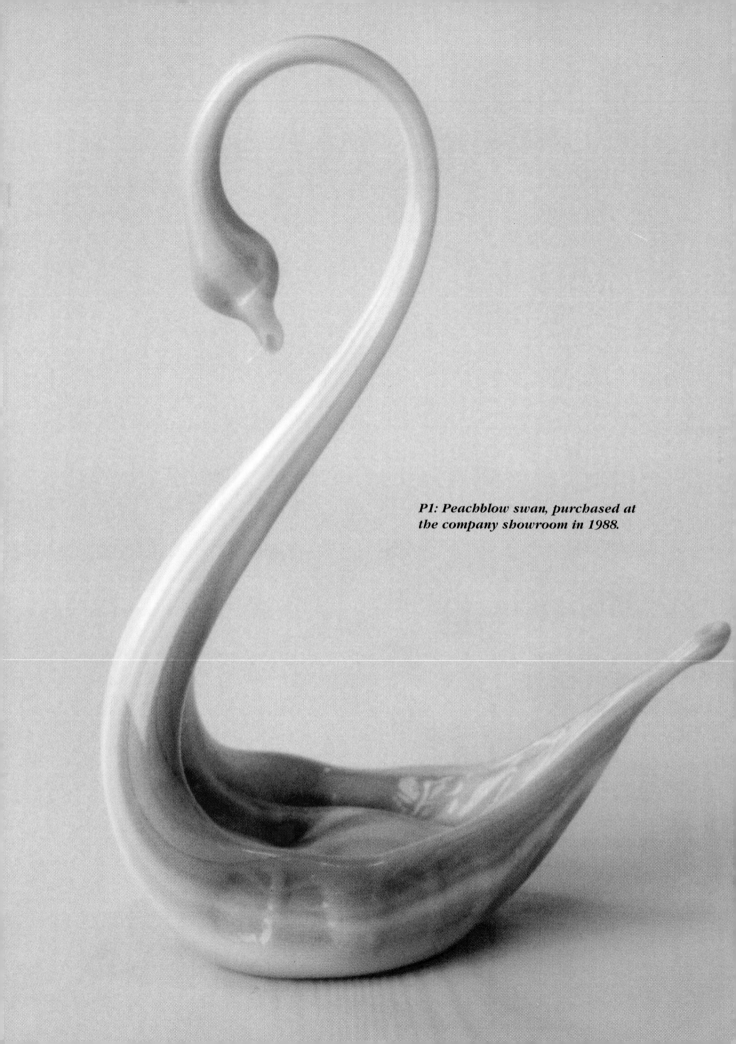

*P1: Peachblow swan, purchased at the company showroom in 1988.*

# Pairpoint Peachblow

Pairpoint is the successor to Gundersen and Gundersen-Pairpoint. The story of Pairpoint peachblow begins with the 1968 release of George C. Avila's book, *The Pairpoint Glass Story*, which created renewed interest in the company that had been one of America's premier glass manufacturers. The firm had been in operation prior to 1970 but had not made glass. Instead, it contracted to have items made in Spain.

The fires at the new glass factory, located in Sagamore, Mass., were lit once again under the direction of Robert Bryden. Because Bryden played such a large part in making the new factory operational, Pairpoint peachblow is sometimes referred to as "Bryden peachblow." In fact, Leonard Padgett refers to it as such in his book, *Pairpoint Glass*, which covers the history of the company up until the date of its publication in 1979.

The firm made peachblow right away because the owners needed money to fund the factory's continued operation. Peachblow was made intermittently for the next 18 years whenever the company needed money. Pairpoint peachblow items were intended to be decorative rather than functional. Most were small, too, so glassmakers could get more items from a pot of glass. Pairpoint was sold in the late 1980s and the current owners have not made peachblow as of this writing. The company's name once again is simply Pairpoint.

*P2: This peachblow glass duck is tiny, standing only about 3" high. It's marked with the P in a diamond trademark.*

### Pairpoint Peachblow Identification Card

**Proper Name:** Peach Blow.

**Manufacturer:** Pairpoint Glass Company, Sagamore, MA.

**Date of Production:** 1970-1988.

**Color:** Most often pink to white. In the late 1970s and early 1980s, some was done with cobalt, resulting in a pink to blue-gray shading.

**Casing:** None.

**Finish:** Both matte and glossy.

**Decorations:** Most often enameled florals, though millefiore designs are found.

**Special Characteristics:** Can have rough or polished pontil. Some pieces will appear cased rather than shaded. This affect was created with an open pot, which did not allow the glass to get hot enough to create the shaded affect. Examples are generally small with large pieces being rare.

*P4: This tiny little pitcher stands only 2-1/4" high.*

*P3: This Pairpoint peachblow bell is desirable because of its paperweight handle and the fact that it was decorated by Cynthia Bryden, wife of Robert Bryden. Not many bells were made, plus Cynthia Bryden didn't do as much decorating as some of the other decorators. The bell was $300 when it was new back in the 1970s. Collection of Louis O. St. Aubin, Jr.*

*P5: A study in contrast—the tiny pitcher shown alongside one of Pairpoint's largest vases.*

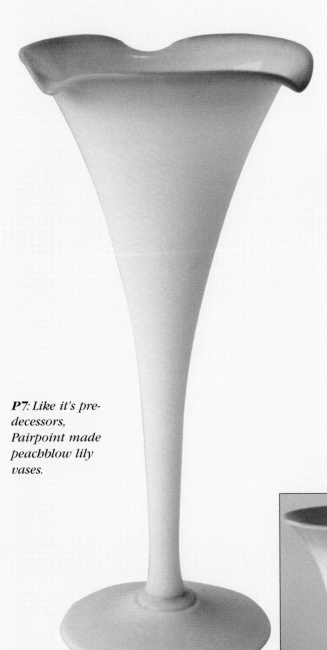

*P7*: Like it's predecessors, Pairpoint made peachblow lily vases.

*P6*: Instead of being decorated with an enamel design added afterwards, this vase is decorated with millefiore.

*P8*: Two trumpet vases.

*P10: The decoration on the hat vase is inside as well as on the rim.*

*P9: Two Pairpoint peachblow hat vases. The larger one was decorated by Cynthia Bryden.*

*P11: A small ruffled vase, which stands only about 3" tall.*

*P12: The decoration on the vase.*

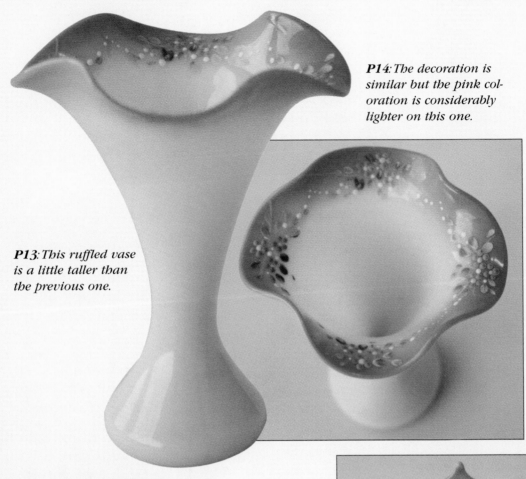

*P14*: The decoration is similar but the pink coloration is considerably lighter on this one.

*P13*: This ruffled vase is a little taller than the previous one.

*P15*: Cynthia Bryden decorated this jack-in-the-pulpit. It stands about 6" tall.

*P16*: This jack is a couple inches taller than the previous one, and has a metal base.

117

*P17:* A plate or shallow bowl decorated by Philip Kiluk.

*P19:* The Pairpoint mark and decorator's signature on the bottom of the basket.

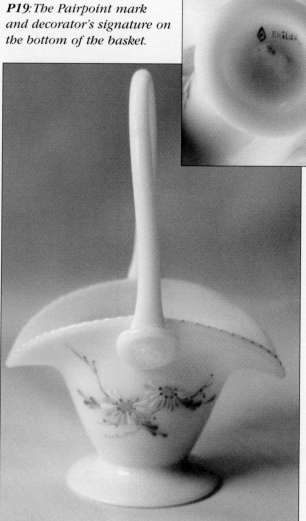

*P18:* A small Pairpoint peachblow glass basket decorated by Philip Kiluk. The glass appears cased, rather than shaded, indicating it was made in an open pot.

*P20:* A small plate or saucer decorated by Philip Kiluk.

*P22*: *This compote was decorated by Philip Kiluk.*

*P21*: *Pairpoint peachblow candlestick.*

*P23*: *A compote.*

*P24*:*An unusual little compote with a ruffled foot as well as a ruffled top.*

*P25*:*A goblet, flower form and small compote, all displaying subtly different colors.*

*P26: A small ruffled vase, with its original label, c. 1988.*

*P27: This photo illustrates the differences between glass made with an open pot (left) and a closed pot. The glass in the closed pot got hot enough to create a shaded effect. Glass from the closed pot appears cased because the glass did not get as hot.*

*P28: This heart-shaped creamer bears a decoration typical of those done in the 1970s.*

*P29: Another creamer, with a bulbous bottom.*

*P31: The pontil mark on the little creamer.*

*P30: And another creamer, shown with a matching sugar bowl. These are tiny, almost child-sized. They were made for decoration, not practical use. Collection of Stu Horn.*

*P32: This group of Pairpoint peachblow vases illustrates the variety in shape, size, decoration and even color.*

***P33**: A variety of Pairpoint peachblow items from the collection of the late Leonard E. Padgett, author of* Pairpoint Glass. *Photo by Bill Pitt, courtesy of Brookside Antiques.*

***P34**: More Pairpoint peachblow items from the collection of the late Leonard E. Padgett, author of* Pairpoint Glass. *Photo by Bill Pitt, courtesy of Brookside Antiques.*

*IT5: This tumbler illustrates the band of purple sometimes found on Italian peachblow. It has a bit of yellow in it, which technically makes it Burmese. But Italian Burmese is often mistaken for peachblow.*

# ❦ CHAPTER 9 ❦

# Italian Peachblow

Murano, an island off the coast of Venice, Italy, has been a glassmaking center for generations. Napoleon nearly put an end to that in the eighteenth century, when his occupation forced most of the glass factories to close. Starting in 1840, the industry began to recover, focusing on making reproductions of antique Venetian glass.

By the twentieth century, the Italians were also reproducing glass originally made outside Venice. It was inevitable that sooner or later, Italian glassmakers would copy peachblow.

In the 1960s and early 1970s, Murano factories began reproducing various types of Victorian art glass. Mother-of-Pearl satin and Burmese are the most prolific of these reproductions. Peachblow was made, but in relatively small quantities. Or, at least it doesn't show up on the secondary market quite as often as reproductions of Burmese and Mother-of-Pearl.

The best copies of peachblow made by the Italians are reproductions of Wheeling peachblow from the 1970s. Cruets, vases and fairy lamps are known, though ruffled top creamers (a shape not originally produced), water pitchers (originally produced), and bowls (exact shape unknown) have been reported. We examined a fairy lamp base, which is shaped like a small spittoon with a flared out and tightly crimped edge. We were surprised how good the colors are! Tool marks are visible on the crimps, though the pontil is polished. It even appeared to have appropriate wear. It would seem likely that the flared pie crust vase would also have tool marks on the crimps, so this is something to look for. In addition, the lining was a bit more stark white than found on originals. And, neither of these shapes were made originally.

Identifying the reproduction ball cruet can be a bit trickier, since this form does imitate an original shape. Original cruets have a trefoil rim, where copies have a cylindrical rim with the spout pulled out on one side. The copies were originally sold with blob-shaped round glass stoppers, but these rarely are found with them when they appear on the secondary market. They've usually been replaced with faceted amber stoppers more closely resembling the originals.

These well-done reproductions offer collectors a way to enjoy an example of the beautiful coloring of Wheeling peachblow at an affordable price. Just be sure not to pay for an original if that's not what you're getting. The only known original Hobbs catalog showing Wheeling peachblow is reprinted in Chapter 3. Studying the shapes found there is one way to learn what was made originally. However, the ball cruet does not appear in the catalog, so we know that the catalog wasn't exhaustive.

Another attempt to copy Wheeling peachblow didn't turn out so well. The color is not a very good copy, resembling a cross between Wheeling peachblow and Imperial peachblow. Toothpicks, tumblers and small creamers are known in both glossy and satin finishes in this line, which also dates to the 1970s. The toothpicks flare out at the top and the bottom, a shape which does not match any of the originals.

Incidentally, a reproduction New England tankard has been reported, though we have not seen one.

A third Italian line appears to have been an attempt to reproduce Mt. Washington peachblow. The glass shades from a rose color to a blue-gray. However, neither the colors nor the glass are as delicate as those found on Mt. Washington. A piece of Mt. Washington peachblow almost looks like someone dusted the piece with dusty rose and blue powder, starting at opposite ends and meeting in the middle. The shading isn't nearly as subtle on these Italian versions. Sometimes the color change is stark, but other times it's more gradual. Still, the delicate affect isn't there. A band of purple is often visible between the pink and the blue-gray. This coloration is not found on Mt. Washington peachblow.

In addition, Italian reproductions of Mt. Washington peachblow are considerably heavier and thicker. Pontils are rough, although they often appear semi-ground, as if an attempt was made merely to make the piece sit level. If the piece is crimped, the crimping tends to be uneven and pointed, and tool marks are often visible. Once you become familiar with this line, it's easy to tell the difference between old and new.

Another type of "peachblow" to show up on the secondary market shades from a cranberry to blue, with both colors being brighter than the peachblow described above. These are decorated with applied glass berries and leaves. None of the Victorian types of peachblow are decorated with any type of applied glass foliage. These pieces are also lined in white. This is an obvious sign that these items are not Washington peachblow because Mt. Washington peachblow was never lined. Like the other type of peachblow discussed above, this type will show tool marks on the crimping and will have rough pontils or poorly formed prunts.

Unfortunately, we have not been able to find an ample supply of Italian peachblow items to include in this book. So, learn to differentiate by studying the colors and shapes of the photos and A.A. Importing catalog pages shown here, and the shapes shown in Chapters 3, 4 and 5.

IT1: *An Italian peachblow rose bowl. This shape is not found on peachblow by Hobbs, Mt. Washington, New England, Gundersen or Pairpoint. Also, note the band of purple around the middle. You won't see this on any other type of peachblow.*

IT2: *An Italian tumbler, this one with an applied flower. Applied foliage is not found on Victorian peachblow.*

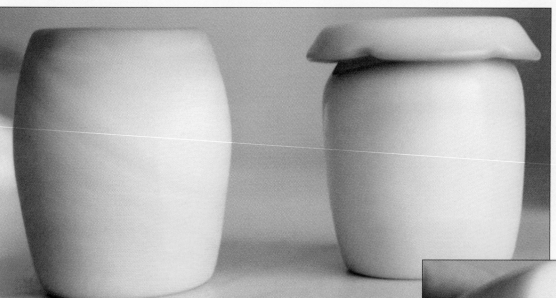

IT3: *Two Italian peachblow toothpick holders. Note the striations of color and the shapes. Courtesy of Grandma Patty's Antiques.*

IT4: *The pontil on this Italian peachblow toothpick holder. Even though it resembles pontil marks sometimes found on Gundersen peachblow, don't confuse the two. Gundersen shades from pink to white.*

*IT6: This catalog page, shown courtesy of A.A. Importing, some of the shapes the Italians produced in Burmese. One of the toothpicks in IT3 is shown on the bottom right of the page, indicating that shapes made in Burmese are also likely to appear in peachblow.*

# "BURMESE"...*the satin glass aristocrat.*

◀ **BU/401 BASKET.** 7½ in. tall. Has applied handle and trim.
Each...**16.50**

**BU/402 CRUET.** 7 in. tall. Matching stopper. Each...**12.50** ▶

**BU/407 FAIRY LAMP.** 5¾ in. tall. 2-piece. Each...**18.50**

**BU/408 CHEESE DISH.** 8¾ in. across. 2-piece. Each...**20.00**

**TOOTHPICK HOLDERS.** 2¼ in. tall.
BU/410 FLARED (Left).
BU/411 OVERLAPPED (Right).
Each...**5.50**

**BU/406 TWO-HANDLE VASE.** 3½ in. tall. Each...**10.50**

**BU/409 GOBLET.** 5¾ in. tall. Each...**10.50**

Page 58  A. A. IMPORTING CO., INC.

# CABINET MASTERPIECES

## HEAVILY APPLIQUED

### *Museum quality choices*

◀ **BU/405 BURMESE MASTER VASE.** 11½ in. tall. Has elaborate "icing" applique. Limited quantity. Each...**37.50**

**BY/403 BURMESE ORNATE VASE.** 8 in. tall. Elaborate "icing" applique. Limited quantity. Each...**28.50**

**IA/2101 CRANBERRY EPERGNE.** Tall 16 in. master display unit. Has three arms with intertwined flowers and crimped base. Each...**42.50**

*IT7: This catalog page shows the epergne found in the cranberry to blue peachblow line, except the peachblow item has applied berries and leaves, rather than applied flowers. A shape very similar to the master floral vase, bottom right, also is found in peachblow, as is a shape similar to the Burmese master vase, top left. It's likely that the other pieces were also made in peachblow. Courtesy of A.A. Importing.*

**SHADED CABINET VASES.** Have elaborate "icing" floral applique. 6⅝ in. tall.
IA/2141 Burgundy shaded to lavender (Left).
IA/2140 Burgundy shaded to white (Right).
Each...**17.50**

**IA/2142 SHADED CABINET CRUET.** 7 in. tall. Matching stopper. Each...**15.00**

**IA/2143 MASTER FLORAL VASE.** 9¼ in. tall. Encircled with 3 floral groupings in applique. Satin amber surface. Cased white inside. Each...**27.50**

A. A. IMPORTING CO., INC.  Page 59

IT8: *A reproduction Wheeling peachblow ball cruet. Compare the spout on this piece to the one shown in* **WH28**. *Photo courtesy of the Burmese Cruet.*

*IT9: Reproduction Wheeling peachblow pie crust vase, which sold for $20 new, and the fairy lamp, which sold for $45 new. Neither of these shapes were made originally. Photo courtesy of the Burmese Cruet.*

### Italian Peachblow Identification Card

**Proper Name:** Unknown
**Manufacturer:** Italian companies located on the island of Murano, off the coast of Venice.
**Date of Production:** 1960s-1970s.
**Color:** Two lines are copies of Wheeling peachblow, and shade from mahogany red to golden orange and islined in white. A second line, apparently created to imitate Mt. Washington peachblow, shades from pink to blue-gray, often with a band of purple in the middle. It is not lined. A third line, which shades from cranberry to blue and is lined in white.
**Casing:** See above.
**Finish:** Both matte and glossy.
**Decorations:** Mt. Washington peachblow copies are sometimes found painted with large flowers.. Lined versions, which shade from cranberry to bright blue, are decorated with applied foliage and berries.
**Special Characteristics:** Once you become accustomed to seeing Italian reproductions of Victorian art glass, you'll notice a certain "look" which will serve as a quick and easy giveaway to their origin. Look for uneven and pointed crimps and evidence of tool marks on the crimps. These charactistics appear on all the Italian glass, even the Wheeling pieces with good color.

*B11: A Bennett peach-blow pitcher.*

# Bennett Peachblow

The story of Bennett peachblow is closely intertwined with that of L.G. Wright. Si Wright, who had been buying peachblow from Salvatore "Sam" Diana, introduced Diana to Harold Bennett. Little did he know that in 1967, Bennett would buy Diana's Rochester, PA glass factory, the Venetian Glass Corp, and the formulas.

"He said 'I'll teach one fellow how to make it,'" Harold Bennett recalls. Bennett became that one fellow. After his teaching work was done, Diana returned to his native Italy, where he died around 1980.

Bennett had all of the glass company equipment and 400 molds moved from Rochester to 609 S. Eighth St. in Cambridge, Ohio, where it was set up as the Guernsey Glass Company, apparently named for the county in which it was located. Bennett still has in his own collection the first piece of peachblow he ever made, a rather awkward looking tumbler. "I put a handle on a piece. I wouldn't want to show it to you, though," he says with a smile.

Bennett employed about 15 people, including skilled glassmakers. Although he made a few of the first pieces of peachblow while learning from Sam Diana, he did not make the glass commercially. His workers did.

Unfortunately Si Wright did himself no favors when he introduced Diana and Bennett. Wright had been buying peachblow items from Diana for $5 apiece, but Bennett refused to sell his peachblow glass for that price. Instead, Bennett and his staff made peachblow items after hours for one or two seasons. They did this after-hours work only in the winter, when it was more comfortable to be near the hot glass furnaces. The items were then sold for $25 each in the factory showroom. Bennett estimates that he made only about 250 pieces.

Most Bennett peachblow is pink to white, often with color striations throughout the body of each piece. However, one of Bennett's workers accidentally produced some which was shaded pink to bluish-gray. He was going to throw out two pieces when Bennett stopped him, saving the only known pieces of what Bennett calls his "Mt. Washington peachblow."

The fact that peachblow was not a big commercial success for Bennett was really no trouble for him because he made his living making pressed glass and glass lamp parts. For him, peachblow was an experimentation in art. He didn't use the white interior casing that Diana did, instead experimenting with different color linings. Some of the approximately 35 peachblow items that he kept for himself have thin amber or green interior casings. Some

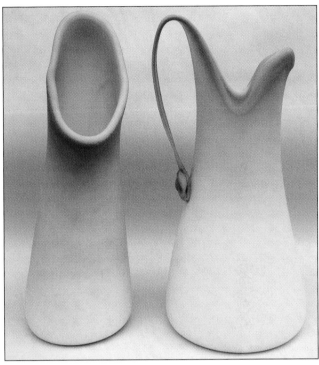

**B2:** *These two pieces were actually mistakes, due to the graying of the color. The workman who made them was going to scrap them, but Bennett said to save them, because the blue-gray coloring reminds him of Mt. Washington peachblow.*

have peachblow handles while other items have colored handles. A number of items have molded patterns in them. Bennett apparently had no list of standard shapes, but instead experimented, making the possible shapes and color variations endless.

One of his workers, Richard Anderson, even took pieces of peachblow cullet home where he heated them and fashioned them into miniature swan figurines. "He could do anything with glass," Bennett says.

Bennett never issued any catalogs for his glass company, nor did he advertise his peachblow. He had one group photo made for Dorothy Hammond, for use in her book, *Confusing Collectibles.* The only other documentation that exists are the approximately 35 items in his own personal collection.

Bennett intended to sign each piece of peachblow he made with his last name, in script. However, most of the pieces in his own collection were not signed, leaving us to wonder how many other items escaped without a signature.

**Bennett Peachblow Identification Card**

**Proper Name:** Peachblow.

**Manufacturer:** Guernsey Glass Company, Cambridge, Ohio.

**Date of Production:** 1968.

**Color:** Generally pink to white.

**Casing:** Not usually. However, some pieces do have a faint white or colored casing.

**Finish:** Both matte and glossy.

**Decorations:** None.

**Special Characteristics:** Some pieces have molded patterns and applied handles of various colors. Some but not all pieces are signed "Bennett" in script. Be careful about calling shaded pink glass "Bennett peachblow." True Bennett peachblow items are quite scarce.

**B1:** *The Guernsey Glass Company as it looks today. Glass has not been made there since 1979, however. Owner Harold Bennett has other companies make glass for him now.*

*B3*: *The first piece of peachblow Harold Bennett made was this tumbler.*

*B4*: *Here are some Bennett peachblow tumblers that turned out a little better!*

*B5*: *Note the rough pontil mark on the bottom of the tumbler.*

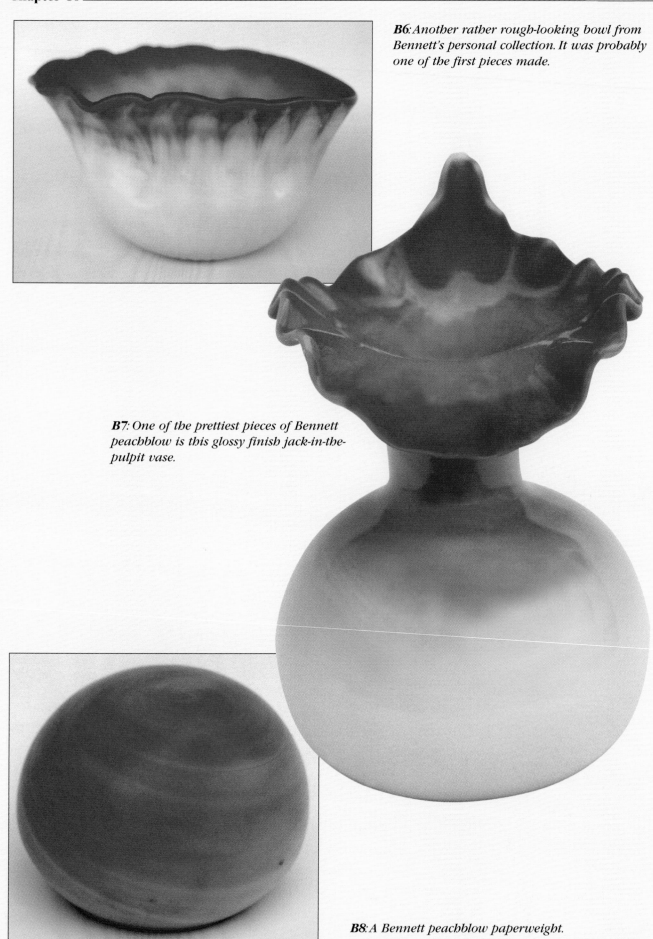

**B6**:*Another rather rough-looking bowl from Bennett's personal collection. It was probably one of the first pieces made.*

**B7**: *One of the prettiest pieces of Bennett peachblow is this glossy finish jack-in-the-pulpit vase.*

**B8**:*A Bennett peachblow paperweight.*

*B9 & B10: Note how different the same shape appears when a pattern is molded into the glass.*

*One of the stickers Bennett used on his glass.*

*B12, B13*, and *B14: Bennett liked to experiment with different colored casings and handles, among other things. Note the subtle differences in these three pitchers, which are shaped the same.*

*B15: A green casing gives this pitcher an unusual effect. Note the pattern in the glass and white handle.*

***B16** and **B17**: Some of the nicest pieces of Bennett peachblow are the large ribbed pitchers which stand about 15" high. Notice how the ribs are more pronounced on one than the other, and how one has a pink handle while the handle on the other is white.*

*The bottom of one
of the pitchers.*

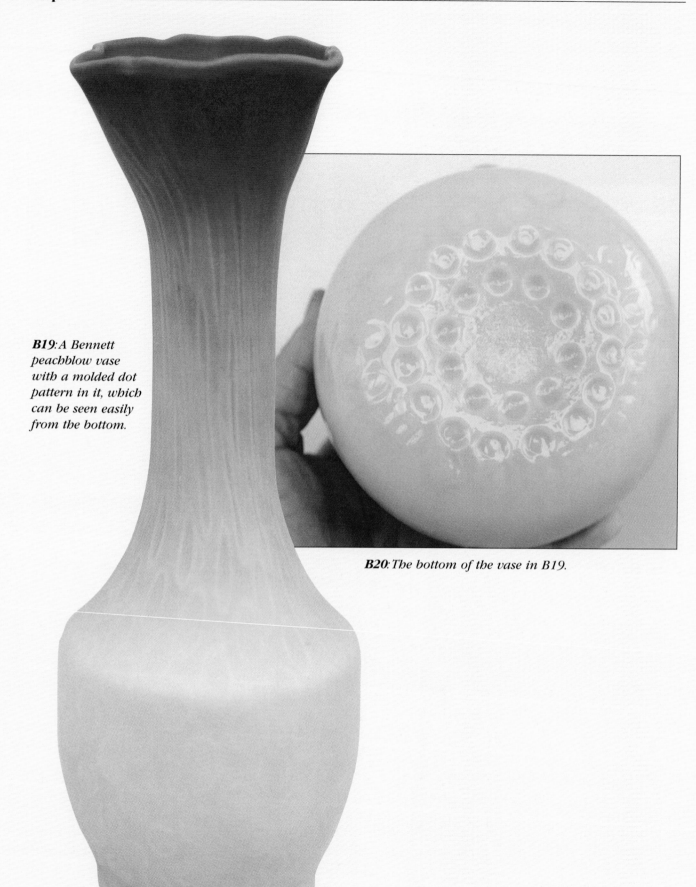

*B19*: *A Bennett peachblow vase with a molded dot pattern in it, which can be seen easily from the bottom.*

*B20*: *The bottom of the vase in B19.*

**B21**: *A peachblow glass bowl made by Sam Diana.*

**B22**: *The same peachblow bowl made by Bennett with a pattern in the glass.*

**B23**: *A staple of Bennett's glass production was lamp ware. This peachblow vase is a modified lamp shade.*

**B24**: *The insert to a Bennett peachblow bride's bowl like the one shown in the group photo on page 143.*

**B25**: *A fancy crimped bowl in peachblow.*

**B27**: *If you didn't know better, you might mistake this piece for Victorian. It is Bennett, however.*

**B26**: *This whimsy is one of a number of pieces in the Bennett home.*

**B28**: *This Bennett peach-blow bell is one of the loveliest pieces in the glassmaker's collection.*

***B29****: A little peachblow cream pitcher in a matte finish with a milk glass handle.*

***B30****: A bulbous bottom vase in a glossy finish.*

***B31****: A Bennett peachblow witch's ball with the hardware and chain to hang it.*

**B32**: *This rose bowl, whose top wasn't turned in, and little vase, are on display in a Cambridge glass museum adjacent to the Bennett home.*

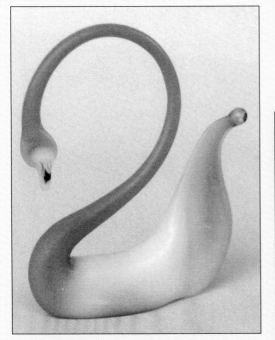

**B33**: *A few pieces of peachblow cullet were saved and made into little swans by Richard Anderson.*

**B34**: *This photograph of Bennett peachblow items was taken for Dorothy Hammond's book,* Confusing Collectibles.

*F4: Persian Medallion rose bowls were made in Fenton's 1915 Peach Blow line. This one, on display at the Fenton factory museum, has a nutmeg spray, rather than a pink "Peach Blow" spray. Examples of items with the pink spray are hard to find. Even the factory storage room is without one.*

# ❦ CHAPTER 11 ❦

# Fenton Peach Blow

Frank M. Fenton has a good memory. That's no surprise really. Still, the tidbit he remembered—that Fenton actually made a line it called "Peach Blow" in 1915—was significant, in light of the fact that most people are more familiar with Fenton's Peach Blow line from 1939.

The 1915 line, produced only for about a year, was a custard glass with a pink spray applied to give it color. Similar green and nutmeg sprays were also used. "I'm just going from memory," he said, as if what he was saying could not be taken as fact. A little digging in his office filing cabinets, and the proof was uncovered—a 1915 catalog page showing 12 different items identified as "Peach Blow Novelty Asst."

**F1**: *The Fenton factory as it stands today.*

Fenton recalls only the pink being considered Peach Blow, yet the catalog page shows both pink and green items. Probably all of these shapes were available with both colors. The catalog shows items in Pond Lily, Sailboats, Butterfly & Berry, Peacock & Dahlia and Blackberry Banded.

There is no price list for the line, but the 1916 inventory list includes some peachblow items, along with prices. On Jan. 1, 1916, Fenton had on hand 60 of the #525 rose bowls (Garlands pattern) in Peach Blow which were priced 60 cents each, 63 of a "new violet vase," which was priced 55 cents each, 15 of the #548 (Persian Medallion) rose bowls priced 55 cents each, and 25 of the #1801 goblets, which were priced $13.25 total. This would indicate that the items produced in this line were not limited to the 12 shapes shown in the catalog page.

The 1939 Fenton Peach Blow line is better known. It consists of a layer of pink (gold ruby glass) inside an outer layer of white. "Peach Blow was our first effort in this type of color," Fenton says, referring to the 1939 line.

Add the crystal edging and the piece is no longer Peach Blow, but Peach Crest. The Peach Blow line lasted only a year, since the Peach Crest treatment proved to be far more

popular. "When we put the crest on it, that kind of took its place," says Fenton. Peach Blow was included in the company price list only in 1939, having been replaced by Peach Crest in 1940.

Although glassmakers were using the name "Peach Blow" to sell their items in the late 1880s, the name had lost its power by the time Fenton began using it. "It probably didn't mean anything to anyone but us," Fenton says.

In 1952, Fenton brought back the Peach Blow color—minus the crystal edging—in a hobnail pattern. But once again, the line was short lived. By 1957, the only piece remaining in the hobnail Peach Blow line was the double crimped hobnail piece, which appears on the back of the 1953-54 catalog.

The company did not keep records of glass made for other companies, but Fenton remembers that the Williamstown firm produced some of the glass for L.G. Wright's line of Peach Blow. Fenton also made Wright's Pink Overlay, which was simply Fenton Peach Blow with the colors reversed.

## Fenton Peachblow Identification Card

**Proper Name:** Peach Blow.

**Manufacturer:** Fenton Art Glass Co., Williamstown, WV.

**Date of Production:** 1915, 1939, 1953-57.

**Color:** The 1915 line is a custard glass with a pink spray around the edges. Green and nutmeg sprays were also used. The 1939 line is white outside with a layer of pink inside. The 1953 line was the same as the 1939 line, only in hobnail.

**Casing:** The 1915 line, no. The 1939 and 1953 lines, yes.

**Finish:** Glossy.

**Decorations:** None.

**Special Characteristics:** It's important to note that Fenton Peach Blow with a crystal edging is not Peach Blow at all, but Peach Crest.

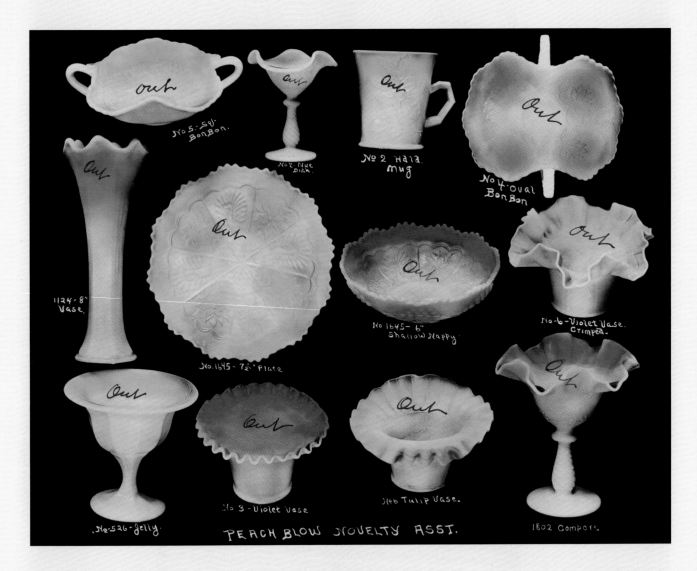

*F2: Except for a few items listed in the Jan. 1, 1916 inventory list, this catalog page from 1915 is the only existing documentation of the 1915 line of Fenton Peach Blow. Courtesy of Frank M. Fenton, Fenton Art Glass Co.*

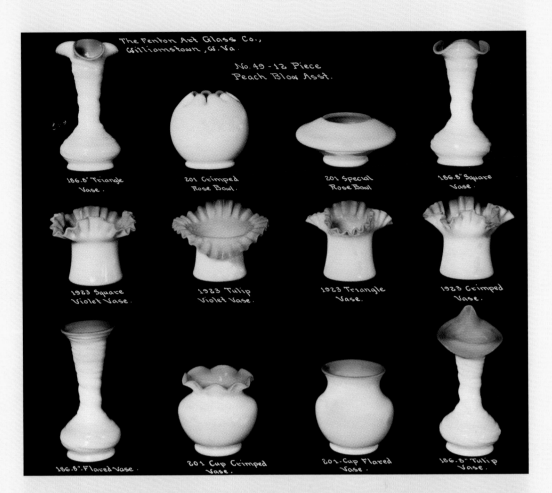

*F3: These two catalog pages from 1939 show the Fenton Peach Blow line most familiar to collectors. Many of these shapes were also produced in Peach Crest. Courtesy of Frank M. Fenton, Fenton Art Glass Co.*

*F6:A Fenton Peach Blow bowl currently in storage at the Fenton factory.*

*F5:A double crimped vase and toothpick in Fenton's 1939 Peach Blow line.*

*F7:The 201 Special Rose Bowl from Fenton's 1939 Peach Blow line. This is one of a number of Peach Blow pieces in storage at the factory.*

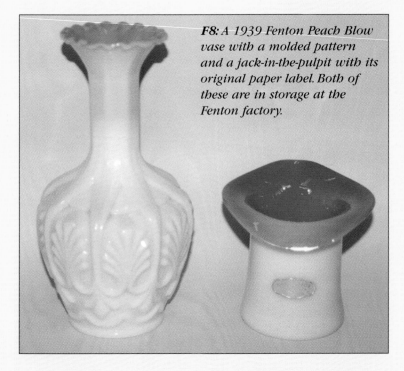

*F8:A 1939 Fenton Peach Blow vase with a molded pattern and a jack-in-the-pulpit with its original paper label. Both of these are in storage at the Fenton factory.*

*F9:A small ribbed handled 1939 Peach Blow pitcher. Courtesy of the Williamstown Antique Mall.*

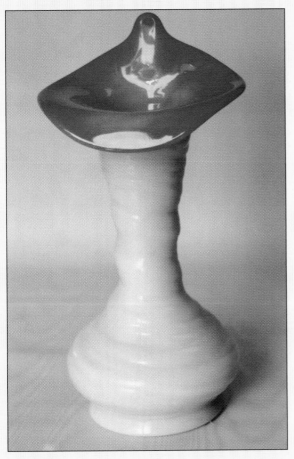

**F10**: *This is Fenton 136 - 8" tulip vase from the 1939 Peach Blow line. This piece is also in storage at the factory.*

**F12**: *This shape is not shown in catalogs, but appears to be a No. 201 cup vase with the "triangle" top shown on the 8" triangle vase, No. 186 in the catalog. See catalog on page 147. Courtesy of the Williamstown Antique Mall.*

**F11**: *This is No. 201 cup flared vase from the 1939 Peach Blow line, also photographed from storage.*

PRICE LIST
of
THE FENTON ART GLASS COMPANY
WILLIAMSTOWN, W. VA.

*1939.*

Plus Package Charge — All Net Prices

PRICE PER DOZEN PIECES

| No. HATS | French Opal | Green Opal | Stiegel Blue | Cran. Red | Blue Ridge | Peach-Blow |
|---|---|---|---|---|---|---|
| *1920—12" Top Hat | $12.00 | $18.00 | $18.00 | $24.00 | $24.00 | |
| 1921—10" Top Hat | 9.00 | 12.00 | 12.00 | 18.00 | 18.00 | |
| 1922— 8" Top Hat | 6.00 | 7.20 | 7.20 | 12.00 | 12.00 | 18.00 |
| 1923— 6" Top Hat | 4.50 | 4.50 | 4.50 | 6.00 | 6.00 | 9.00 |
| *1924— 4" Top Hat | 2.40 | 3.60 | 3.60 | 4.50 | 4.50 | 6.00 |
| **HANDLED BASKETS** | | | | | | |
| 1921—11" Basket | | | | 24.00 | 24.00 | |
| 1922—10" Basket | | 12.00 | | 18.00 | 18.00 | 24.00 |
| 1923— 6" Basket | 7.20 | | | 9.00 | 9.00 | |
| *1924— 4½" Basket | | | | 6.00 | | |
| 201— 9" Basket | | | | 12.00 | 12.00 | |
| **BOWL AND VASES** | | | | | | |
| 183—10" Vases—Regular, Flared, Triangular, Square and Special | 7.20 | | 9.00 | 12.00 | 12.00 | |
| 186—8" Vases—Flared, Tulip, Triangular | 4.50 | 4.50 | 4.50 | 6.00 | 6.00 | 9.00 |
| *187—7" Vases—Flared, Triangular, Crimped | 9.00 | | | 18.00 | 18.00 | 24.00 |
| º188—7" Flared, 9½" Flared, 7½" Cupped | 9.00 | | | 18.00 | 18.00 | |
| 201—Bowl—Cupped, Flared, Cup-Crimped and Special | 4.50 | 4.50 | 4.50 | 6.00 | 6.00 | 9.00 |
| *893—Ginger Jar, Base, Cover | 9.00 | | 12.00 | 18.00 | | |
| 894—10" Vase—Tulip, Flared, Triangular | 7.20 | | 9.00 | 12.00 | 12.00 | |
| 895—10" Flared Vase | | | 9.00 | 12.00 | 12.00 | |
| 1522—Bowls and Bases—Flared, Oval, Crimped, Triangular, Square | 7.20 | 7.20 | 9.00 | 9.00 | 9.00 | |
| 1522—Bowl only—above shapes | | | | | | 15.00 |
| 1522—Block—White, $1.50 | | | | | | |
| 1522—Nymph—White, $1.50 | | | | | | |
| 1522—Base—White, $1.50 | | | | | | |
| 1522—4-piece Nymph Set—Crimped or Flared | 10.80 | 10.80 | 10.80 | 12.00 | 12.00 | 19.50 |
| 1523—12" Flared Bowl | | | | 24.00 | 24.00 | |
| 1523—Candleholders (Dozen Pairs) | 9.00 | | | 12.00 | 12.00 | |
| 1922—B Vases—Flared, Triangular, Square | 7.20 | 7.20 | 9.00 | 12.00 | 12.00 | 18.00 |
| **BEVERAGE SETS AND LAMPS** | | | | | | |
| 187—7-pc. Beverage Set (with 9-oz. Tumblers) | 18.00 | | | 36.00 | 36.00 | |
| 187—9-pc. Beverage Set (with 9-oz. Tumblers) | 21.00 | | | 42.00 | 42.00 | |
| 187—7-pc. Beverage Set (with 12-oz. Tumblers) | 19.50 | | | 37.50 | 37.50 | |
| 187—9-pc. Beverage Set (with 12-oz. Tumblers) | 23.00 | | | 44.00 | 44.00 | |
| 187—9-oz. Tumbler only | 1.50 | | | 3.00 | 3.00 | |
| 187—12-oz. Tumbler only | 1.75 | | | 3.25 | 3.25 | |
| *1352—7-pc. Beverage Set (with 12-oz. Tumblers) | 15.00 | 15.00 | | | | |
| *1352—7-pc. Beverage Set (with 9-oz. Tumblers) | | | | 36.00 | | |
| 170—Hurricane Lamp and Base (Bases in Crystal, Milk and Matt Crystal) | 7.20 | 7.20 | 7.20 | 10.80 | 10.80 | |

*Not illustrated. (Prices indicate the color in which the items are made.)

**F13**: *The 1939 Fenton price list includes items from the Peach Blow line, all of which came in a number of other colors. Courtesy of Frank M. Fenton, Fenton Art Glass Co.*

THE FENTON ART GLASS COMPANY, WILLIAMSTOWN, W. VA.

*F14: In 1952, Fenton introduced its Peach Blow coloring in hobnail. This is probably the most well-known and often seen hobnail Peach Blow piece since it was the only one to remain in the line until 1957. This piece is in storage at the factory.*

*F15: The back of the 1953-54 Fenton catalog shows the hobnail Peach Blow item shown in the previous photograph. Courtesy of Frank M. Fenton, Fenton Art Glass Co.*

*F16: Fenton company records include this price list for Peach Blow hobnail. It's undated, but since it includes a variety of pieces, it is probably one of the older Peach Blow hobnail price lists. Courtesy of Frank M. Fenton, Fenton Art Glass Co.*

**Fenton Art Glass Co.**     Customer:

Actual No. Pcs. Each Color

| CATALOG PAGE NO. | QUANTITY DOZ. | STYLE NO. | **PEACH BLOW HOBNAIL** SIZE AND DESCRIPTION | PEACH BLOW | PRICE Per Doz. | FW'D TOTAL / TOTAL | Mfr's. Suggested Retail Price Per Item |
|---|---|---|---|---|---|---|---|
| 3 | | 389 | 3" DC Vase | | 9.00 | | 1.50 |
| 4 | | 389 | 6" Bonbon | | 6.00 | | 1.00 |
| 4 | | 389 | 7" Handled Basket | | 18.00 | | 3.00 |
| 4 | | 389 | 10" Handled Basket | | 30.00 | | 5.00 |
| 5 | | 389 | Miniature Vase | | 6.00 | | 1.00 |
| 5 | | 389 | 7" Bowl | | 12.00 | | 2.00 |
| 5 | | 389 | 9" Bowl | | 15.00 | | 2.50 |
| 6 | | 389 | 5 1/2" Handled Basket | | 10.50 | | 1.75 |
| 8 | | 389 | 4 1/2" Vase | | 12.00 | | 2.00 |
| 8 | | 389 | 5" Vase | | 15.00 | | 2.50 |
| 8 | | 389 | 6" Vase | | 15.00 | | 2.50 |
| | | 389 | Hurricane Chimney and Handled Base | | 22.50 | | 3.75 |

| CATALOG PAGE NO. | QUANTITY DOZ. | STYLE NO. | **HOBNAIL** SIZE AND DESCRIPTION | MILK | GREEN | PRICE Per Doz. | FW'D TOTAL / TOTAL | Mfr's. Suggested Retail Price Per Item |
|---|---|---|---|---|---|---|---|---|
| | | 389 | 6" Jardiniere | | | 6.00 | | 1.00 |
| | | 389 | 4 1/2" Jardiniere | | | 4.80 | | .80 |

TOTAL

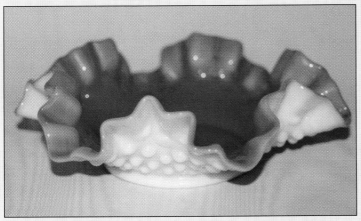

*F17:* This Peach Blow hobnail item also shows up fairly often. This one is from the Fenton factory storage room.

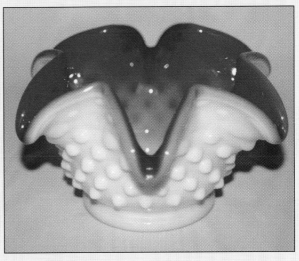

*F18:* This small piece has a very pretty star shaped opening. It is from the factory storage room.

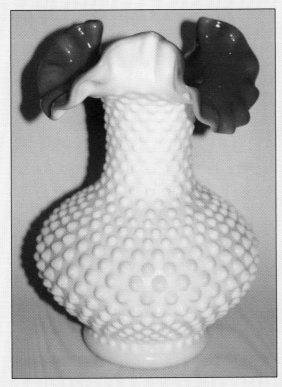

*F19:* A Fenton Peach Blow vase with a "triangle" top, from the factory storage room.

*F20:* This Fenton shape is found fairly frequently, but seldom in Peach Blow. This one, from the 1950s line, came from the factory storage room.

*F21:* A two-piece Fenton hobnail lamp. Courtesy of the Williamstown Antique Mall.

*LGW3: The L.G. Wright Glass Co. was known for its glass lamps. This Peach Blow example is painted with the moss rose decoration. Item photographed courtesy of the Williamstown Antique Mall, Williamstown, WV.*

# ❦ CHAPTER 12 ❦

# L.G. Wright Peach Blow

The L.G. Wright Glass Company of New Martinsville, WV, never made its own glass, but instead contracted with other glass companies to make glass from Wright's molds. Two companies are known to have made glass for the line Wright called "Peach Blow." One is the Fenton Art Glass Co. of Williamstown, WV, and the other is the Venetian Glass Co. of Rochester, PA.

*LGW1: The former L.G. Wright Glass Factory as it stands today.*

Wright was a shrewd businessman. Authors James Measell and W.C. "Red" Rotteis say in their book, *The L.G. Wright Glass Company*, that company owner Lawrence Gale "Si" Wright often went from factory to factory, ordering glass wherever he could get the best price. Frank M. Fenton remembers this and how it came to play in the manufacturer of Wright's Peach Blow line.

Apparently Fenton had begun making Wright peachblow. "But I think Si (Wright) found a whole lot better price with Sam," recalls Fenton. Wright tracked down Salvatore "Sam" Diana, owner of the Venetian Glass Corp., in about 1953 and began buying Peach Blow items there for $5 apiece. "His color was different than ours, but Si was able to get by with it," Fenton says.

Some years later, Diana asked Fenton for a job. "He said, 'If I come to work for you, then you'll have all the knowledge that I have and you can charge Mr. Wright anything you want to,'" Fenton remembers. Fenton didn't hire him, though, and in 1967 Diana sold his factory to Harold Bennett.

Wright's peachblow comes in two color schemes. The first is a heat sensitive glass that shades from pink to white and has a white lining. The second is white glass over an interior layer of pink. The Peach Blow color appeared in the Beaded Curtain and Maize patterns, in lamps such as Embossed Rose, and was made in a variety of shapes with no specific pattern. These were often decorated with the Moss Rose pattern, inspired by decorated china and actually applied to the glass by the Zarilla Art Glass Co. of Rochester, PA. Wright eventually decorated its own glass, but did not start its decorating department until 1968.

The peachblow coloring in the Beaded Curtain pattern includes lamp shades and fonts, a pickle castor insert, a tumbler, rose bowl, creamer, sugar, spooner and pitcher.

In Maize, the Peach Blow color scheme is found in rose bowls, lamp shades and fonts.

*LGW2: The company closed in May 1999.*

Peach Blow lamps are also found in the Embossed Rose pattern, as is a rose bowl with no crimps.

The other shapes — which don't have any kind of pattern — in which Peach Blow is found include rose bowls, cruets, pickle jars, crimped finger bowls, tumblers, creamers, fairy lamps, pickle castors, pitchers, and vases including the "picture vase," which has a flat round surface. The color is also sometimes found on cherry pattern vases, some of which are painted.

The heat sensitive Peach Blow, with shaded pink to white glass over a white casing, is found in rose bowls, barber bottles, and vases made from the barber bottles. Incidentally, the heat sensitive pieces were not decorated. Rotteis said he had some decorated for his own use and that refiring the decorations for permanence caused a darkening of the pink color.

It's important to note that when the pink color outside is not shaded, Wright did not call it Peach Blow. The term Peach Blow was used only when the pink layer was inside, or when it was a heat-sensitive formula. When the outside color is uniform, the company called it "pink overlay" or "rose overlay" for the darker version.

---

**L.G. Wright Peachblow Identification Card**

**Proper Name:** Peach Blow.

**Manufacturer:** Venetian Glass Corp. of Rochester, PA and the Fenton Art Glass Co. of Williamstown, WV produced this line for the L.G. Wright Glass Co. of New Martinsville, WV.

**Date of Production:** 1950s-1967.

**Color:** Shaded pink to white, or white with pink interior.

**Casing:** Yes. The shaded pink to white version has a white interior.

**Finish:** Both matte and glossy.

**Decorations:** Often found with "Moss Rose" decoration.

**Special Characteristics:** Although the Moss Rose decoration is the most prevalent painted decoration, it is not the only one. On some pieces, such as those in Embossed Rose, the decoration is the pattern.

---

*LGW4: Three or four dozen Wright Peach Blow rose bowls were offered for sale when the company liquidated in May 1999. They averaged $45 to $60 apiece.*

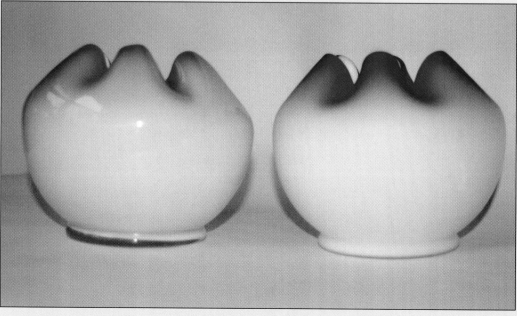

*LGW5: Both Fenton and Diana made Wright Peach Blow rose bowls like these, in the smaller of the two known Wright rose bowl shapes. Note the matte and glossy finishes.*

**LGW6:** *Wright Peach Blow rose bowls with moss rose decoration. Note the variation in size. Collection of Stu Horn.*

**LGW7:** *Notice how the pink interior lining is found only around the top edge on this Wright Peach Blow rose bowl. Collection of Stu Horn.*

**LGW8:** *Wright Peach Blow items are sometimes found undecorated. Collection of Stu Horn.*

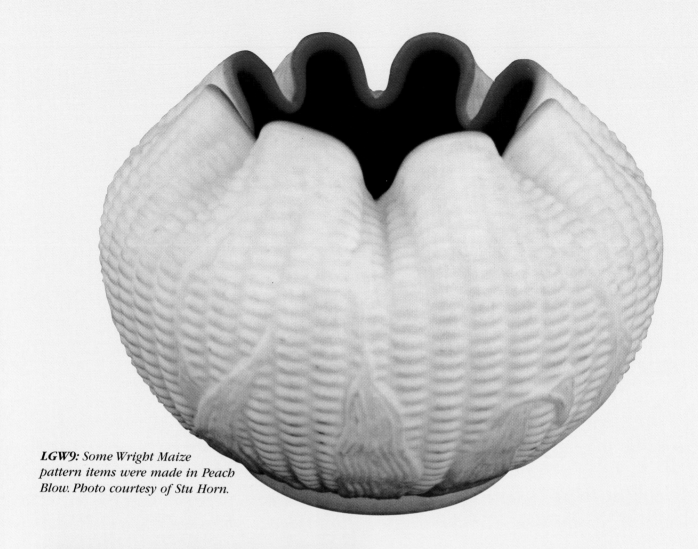

***LGW9:*** *Some Wright Maize pattern items were made in Peach Blow. Photo courtesy of Stu Horn.*

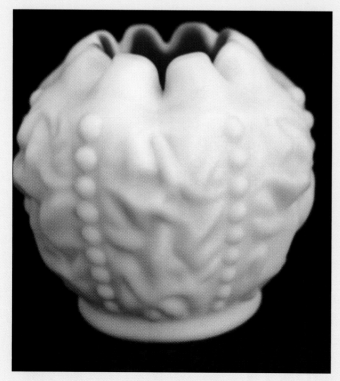

***LGW10:*** *A Wright Peach Blow rose bowl in the beaded curtain pattern. Collection of Stu Horn.*

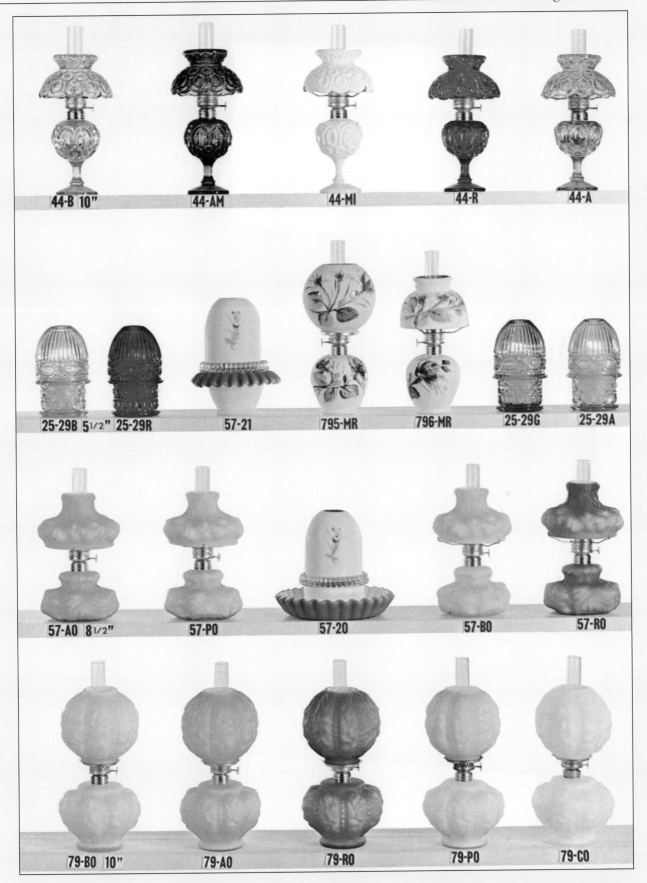

44-B 10"  44-AM  44-MI  44-R  44-A

25-29B 5½"  25-29R  57-21  795-MR  796-MR  25-29G  25-29A

57-AO 8½"  57-PO  57-20  57-BO  57-RO

79-BO 10"  79-AO  79-RO  79-PO  79-CO

**LGW11**: *This L.G. Wright catalog supplement page shows two fairy lamps (second row, third item; third row, middle) and two miniature lamps (second row, fourth and fifth items) in the Peach Blow line. Courtesy of West Virginia Museum of American Glass archives.*

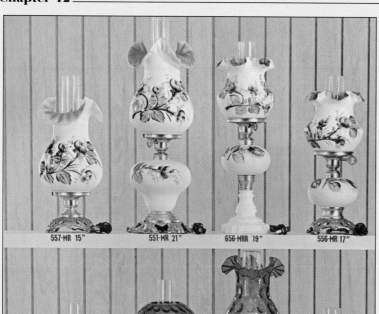

557-MR 15"    551-MR 21"    656-MRR 19"    556-MR 17"

69-1CR 22"    553-1 25"    552-1 27"

*LGW12: A catalog page showing an assortment of Peach Blow lamps, decorated with the moss rose pattern, from the Wright line. Courtesy of West Virginia Museum of American Glass archives.*

725-5CR 11"    558-1 12"    556-3 17"    558-MR 12"    725-2CR 11"

751-MR 21"    917-RS 23"    1001-1CR 25"    551-2 21"

*LGW13: This catalog page shows a Wright Peach Blow shade, decorated with the moss rose pattern, paired with a Beaded Curtain font (bottom, left). A smaller lamp with a Peach Blow shade is shown on the top row, second from right. Courtesy of West Virginia Museum of American Glass archives.*

*LGW14: Wright Peach Blow was apparently made extensively in lamps. The embossed rose pattern includes a Peach Blow lamp (bottom, right). Courtesy of West Virginia Museum of American Glass archives.*

*LGW15: Another embossed rose lamp in Peach Blow, this one in a different style. Courtesy of West Virginia Museum of American Glass archives.*

*LGW16: And a third style in Peach Blow Embossed Rose lamps. Courtesy of West Virginia Museum of American Glass archives.*

*LGW17: And one more Embossed Rose lamp style to be found in Peach Blow. Courtesy of West Virginia Museum of American Glass archives.*

*LGW18:* Don't confuse Wright Peach Blow (third row, second from right) with the many items found in pink overlay shown on this page. Courtesy of West Virginia Museum of American Glass archives.

**Beautiful "WRIGHT GLASS"**
Our Custard Glass, truly, replicas of rare by-gone days.

*LGW19:* This page, from the 1969 catalog supplement, shows a Peach Blow cruet and tall cream pitcher. Courtesy of West Virginia Museum of American Glass archives.

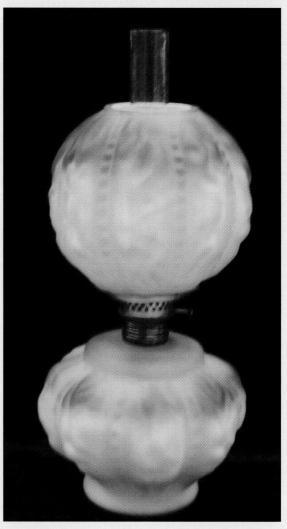

**LGW20**: *An L.G. Wright Peach Blow mini lamp in the beaded curtain pattern. The company called these "toy lamps." This particular peach-blow coloration is called "opal cased." The exterior is shaded. The interior layer is white. Photo courtesy of Stu Horn.*

**LGW21**: *A miniature lamp in Peach Blow with Moss Rose decoration. Wright catalogs referred to the tiny lamps as both miniature and "toy" lamps. Courtesy of Sara Sampson Antiques.*

*LGW22: An undecorated Wright Peach Blow tumbler. Courtesy of GlimmerGlass Antiques.*

*LGW23: A Peach Blow rose bowl in the Embossed Rose pattern. Photo courtesy of Debbie and Cliff Lacey.*

*LGW24: L.G. Wright Peach Blow fairy lamp. Photo courtesy of Bob & Marjorie McCleskey.*

*IM2: Vases 4036 and 4037 both were shaped like these, only 4036 was 8 -3/4" tall, while 4037 was 10-1/2" tall.*

## ❦ CHAPTER 13 ❦

# Imperial Peachblow

The Imperial Glass Corporation of Bellaire, Ohio, introduced the first three matte vases in its Peachblow line on Jan. 1, 1964. Three more vases in a matte finish, which the company called "velvet," would follow in July of that year. The glossy finish, which the company called "plain," was introduced a year later, along with the addition of stoppers in two of its six shapes. All eight shapes would be discontinued Dec. 31, 1967.

Imperial wanted to capture the mystique associated with Victorian peachblow and sought to copy the Hobbs, Brockunier line. An ad, which apparently dates to July or August of 1964, reads as follows:

No late 19th Century Glass Ware showed more skill, artistry and beauty than Peachblow. The first Wheeling Peachblow was made in 1886 by Wm. Leighton, Jr. This item was copied from a famed one-of-its-kind Chinese Porcelain called Peachblow, known as the Morgan vase— named after its owner, Mary J. Morgan. Leighton's Peachblow was an exact copy of the Morgan vase in shape and color, from the deepest ruby to a delicate yellow-green. Imperial's reproductions are based on long research and trials. The basic methods are those of 1886, so these Genuine Peachblow Vases are truly proud achievements. Each of the six Peachblow shapes (three are new and have never been shown before) has an attached story tag.

Not surprisingly, company advertising didn't get all the facts right, but then the ad was designed to sell vases, not document history.

The shading of Imperial Peachblow is considerably different from Wheeling, but the basic colors are correct. It shades from a dark red to a lighter red to a golden yellow and then back to red again, and is cased with milk glass. On some pieces, the body of the vessel is white, separating two bands of golden yellow. On others, no white is found. Carl Gustkey, who was Imperial's president at the time, did attempt to get the colors just right, and he was often impatient when problems developed. Gustkey felt many of these pieces had too much white, according to Lucile Kennedy, who served for years as Imperial's marketing manager. Production and marketing engaged in many discussions regarding the issue of color control.

Imperial Peachblow story tags make historical errors similar to those in the ad. One side of the tag shows a silhouette of Imperial's Morgan vase along with the words "Genuine Peachblow" and "Handcrafted Cased Glass Circa 1886." The text, clearly designed to promote the company, reads:

The Handcrafted Skills necessary to accomplish the Imperial Reproduction of "Wheeling Peachblow" are based on long, tedious research and trials. They attest to Imperial's proud position as The House of Americana Glassware. Basically our Peachblow methods are those of 1868. Raw Materials today are unlike those of a hundred years ago, Melting Vessels and Fuels are different and Skills are not the same, so these GENUINE PEACHBLOW VASES are proud achievements! Gifts from Imperial always have Heritage, each one a "story" and they weave simplicity, antiquity and uniquity into lovely, decorative and useful articles for Gracious Living.

Inside, the tag says:

Of the late 19th century glass "Fancy Wares," none exemplified greater artistry, beauty and skill than Peachblow. Genuine "originals" are extremely rare today! In 1868 William Leighton Jr., of Hobbs, Brockunier & Company (operating a factory started in 1845) made the first *Wheeling Peachblow* and the item was a Vase copied from a famed one-of-its-kind Chinese Porcelain called Peachblow, known as the "Morgan vase" and named after its then-owner Mary J. Morgan. This Porcelain brought $18,000 at public auction back in 1886 at New York City. Quite a price! it was only 8" tall and is profiled on the face of this Story-Brochure. Leighton's Peachblow glass vase was an exact copy of the Morgan Porcelain, both in shape AND color. One of these 1868 Hobbs Brockunier *Originals* is in the J. Ralph Boyd Memorial Glass Collection of the Mansion Museum, Oglebay Park, Wheeling, West Virginia, where it is on public exhibit. It was made by gathering "Gold Ruby" Glass over a Milk Glass "gob" and this procedure was and still is called "casing" or "plating." The Pipe-blown Vase was then carefully heat-struck in a fiery Glory Hole to get the genuine *Wheeling Peachblow* characteristic—exquisite color-shading from deepest Ruby to a delicate yellow-green.

Where the date of 1868 came from is unclear, since the Morgan vase was not sold until 1886, at which time the peachblow hoopla began. There is no evidence to suggest that Leighton was working on peachblow, or copying this vase, prior to the auction. The line now known as Wheeling peachblow had been developed before the auction, but not by 18 years! Maybe the last two digits were transposed.

What follows is a listing of the items in the Imperial Peachblow line, according to when they were introduced. Retail prices at introduction and, when known, when discontinued, appear after the item description. The shapes added in 1965 were apparently added so retail outlets could offer a more striking display, and thereby, sell more vases.

*Introduced Jan. 1, 1964, all in satin finish*
#163, 8" vase, $6-$7.50 retail
#4036, 8.75" vase, $6-$7.50 retail
#4037, 10.5" vase, $7-$8.50

*Introduced July 31, 1964, all in satin finish*
#980, 7.75" vase, $7-$8.50
#983, 9.5" vase, flared bottom, $7-$8.50
#4038, Morgan vase, $7-$8.50

*Introduced July 1, 1965, in both plain and satin finishes. Plain finish now available on previously introduced items.*
#4038/1, decanter and stopper (Morgan vase shape), both finishes, $9
# 980/1, decanter and stopper (bulbous bottom) $9

---

### Imperial Peachblow Identification Card

**Proper Name:** Peachblow.

**Manufacturer:** Imperial Glass Corporation of Bellaire, OH.

**Date of Production:** 1964-1967.

**Color:** Shades from dark red to lighter red to golden yellow and then back to dark red again, often with a band of white around the middle.

**Casing:** Yes, white.

**Finish:** Both matte and glossy.

**Decorations:** None.

**Special Characteristics:** Line includes 8 shapes, all standing between 7.75" and 10.5" plus two of these shapes were also made with stoppers.

---

*IM1: This matte finished vase on the left was introduced by Imperial when its Peachblow line debuted Jan. 1, 1964. It originally retailed for $6, and was discontinued at the end of 1967, when it retailed for $7.50. The glossy finish, which Imperial called "plain," was introduced in 1965.*

*IM3: Vase No. 980, left, which stands 7-3/4" tall, was introduced in July 1964. The version with the stopper, No. 980/1, was introduced a year later. The stoppered version retailed for $2 more than the one without the stopper.*

**IM4:** *Imperial's Morgan vase was first introduced in July 1964 in a satin finish. The plain or glossy finish wasn't introduced in this line for another year, when the shape was also introduced with a stopper, and referred to as a "decanter and stopper." Without the stopper, it is item #4038. The addition of "/1" to the item No. indicates it has a stopper.*

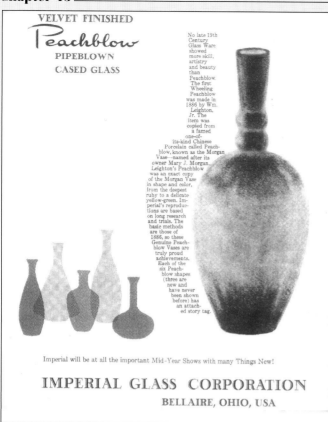

**IM5:** *This ad, which dates to late 1964, advertises the first six shapes in Imperial Peachblow. Courtesy of Cliff McCaslin, National Imperial Glass Collectors Society.*

**IM6:** *This framed photograph was given to salesmen in 1964. Courtesy of Cliff McCaslin, National Imperial Glass Collectors Society.*

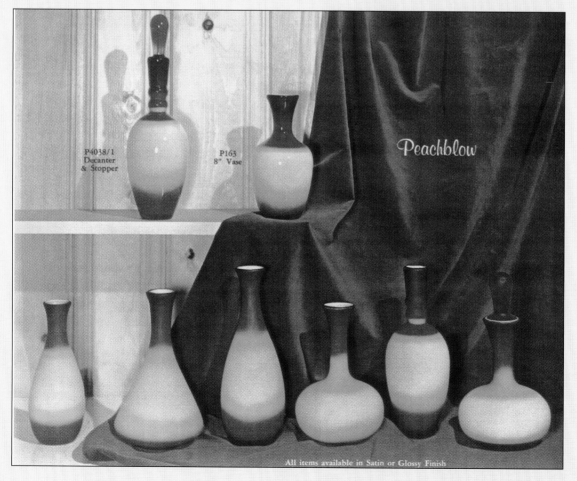

**IM7:** *This page from Imperial's 1966A catalog, published in 1967, shows all eight shapes in Imperial's Peachblow line. Courtesy of Cliff McCaslin, National Imperial Glass Collectors Society.*

IM8: *The story tag, which accompanied each piece of new Imperial Peachblow, came in both tan and peach. This one is shown courtesy of Joan Cimini of the National Imperial Glass Collectors Society.*

IMPERIAL GLASS CORPORATION
BELLAIRE, OHIO, USA

Gracious Living.

ative and useful articles for
uniquity into lovely, decor-
weave simplicity, antiquity and
each one a "story," and they
Imperial always have Heritage,
proud achievements! Gifts from
GENUINE PEACHBLOW VASES are
are not the same, so these
Fuels are different and Skills
years ago, Melting Vessels and
are unlike those of a hundred
of 1868. Raw Materials today
our Peachblow methods are those
Americana Glassware. Basically
position as The House of
They attest to Imperial's proud
tedious research and trials.
*Peachblow,*" are based on long,
Reproductions of "*Wheeling
to accomplish the Imperial
The Handcrafted Skills necessary

## GENUINE
### Velvet Finished
## PEACHBLOW

### Handcrafted
### Cased Glass

CIRCA
1868

AUTHENTIC
AMERICANA
BY
IMPERIAL

OF THE LATE 19TH CENTURY GLASS "Fancy Wares" none exemplified greater artistry, beauty and skill than Peachblow. Genuine "originals" are EXTREMELY rare today! In 1868 William Leighton, Jr., of Hobbs, Brockunier & Company, (operating a factory started in 1845) made the first *Wheeling Peachblow* and the item was a Vase copied from a famed one-of-its-kind Chinese Porcelain called Peachblow, known as the "Morgan Vase" and named after its then-owner Mary J. Morgan. This Porcelain-brought $18,000 at public auction back in 1886 at New York City. Quite a price! It was only 8″ tall and is profiled on the face of this Story-Brochure.

LEIGHTON'S PEACHBLOW GLASS VASE was an EXACT copy of the Morgan Porcelain, both in shape AND color. One of these 1868 Hobbs, Brockunier *Originals* is in the J. Ralph Boyd Memorial Glass Collection of the Mansion Museum, Oglebay Park, Wheeling, West Virginia, where it is on public exhibit. It was made by gathering "Gold Ruby" Glass over a Milk Glass "gob" and this procedure was and still is called "casing," or "plating." The Pipe-blown Vase was then carefully heat-struck in a fiery Glory Hole to get the genuine *Wheeling Peachblow* characteristic—exquisite color-shading from deepest Ruby to a delicate yellow-green.

IM9: *An original Imperial Peachblow sticker, shown considerably larger than actual size. Courtesy of Joan Cimini of the National Imperial Glass Collectors Society.*

CIRCA 1868 PEACHBLOW BY IMPERIAL

**PIL4: This is one of the miniature pitchers shown in the catalog.**

# ❦ CHAPTER 14 ❦

# Pilgrim Peachblow

The Pilgrim Glass Co. of Ceredo, WV was founded in 1956 by Alfred E. Knobler. From the beginning, the company specialized in free blown glass in vivid colors, especially crackle glass. It's probably best known for its cranberry glass, introduced in 1968. It's been such a success that it is still a staple product today.

Pilgrim got in on the peachblow action in 1969, when the firm introduced its "Peachblow," a shaded reddish orange to yellow with a greenish cast.

Pilgrim peachblow items come in two sizes. Those designated as "miniatures" are small pitchers which stand between three and four inches tall. Only six shapes appear in the catalog as "peachblow miniatures," but the peachblow color is found in other Pilgrim miniature shapes too. The larger size consists of about 11 different decanters and a compote. Apples and pears are also shown in this color in the 1969 catalog.

*PIL1: The Pilgrim factory as it stands today.*

How long Pilgrim made peachblow is uncertain. It appears in catalogs until the late 1970s, but may have been made even a bit longer.

---

### Pilgrim Peachblow Identification Card

**Proper Name:** Peachblow

**Manufacturer:** Pilgrim Glass Co., Ceredo, WV.

**Date of Production:** 1969-1978. Other dates possible.

**Color:** Shades from reddish-orange to greenish yellow.

**Casing:** None.

**Finish:** Matte.

**Decorations:** None.

**Special Characteristics:** Most pieces will have rough pontil marks. Some items will have frosted clear handles. Shapes are similar to those found in Kanawha peachblow, but the colors are quite different.

---

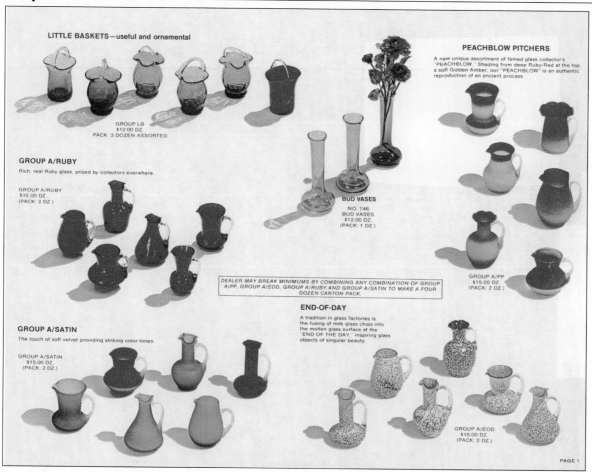

LITTLE BASKETS—useful and ornamental

GROUP LB
$12.00 DZ
PACK: 3 DOZEN ASSORTED

**GROUP A/RUBY**

Rich, real Ruby glass, prized by collectors everwhere.

GROUP A/RUBY
$15.00 DZ.
(PACK: 2 DZ.)

**GROUP A/SATIN**

The touch of soft velvet providing striking color tones.

GROUP A/SATIN
$15.00 DZ.
(PACK: 2 DZ.)

PEACHBLOW PITCHERS

A new unique assortment of famed glass collector's "PEACHBLOW." Shading from deep Ruby-Red at the top, a soft Golden Amber, our "PEACHBLOW" is an authentic reproduction of an ancient process.

BUD VASES

NO. 746
BUD VASES
$12.00 DZ.
(PACK: 1 DZ.)

DEALER MAY BREAK MINIMUMS BY COMBINING ANY COMBINATION OF GROUP A/PP, GROUP A/EOD, GROUP A/RUBY AND GROUP A/SATIN TO MAKE A FOUR DOZEN CARTON PACK.

**END-OF-DAY**

A tradition in glass factories is the fusing of milk glass chips into the molten glass surface at the "END OF THE DAY," inspiring glass objects of singular beauty.

GROUP A/PP
$15.00 DZ.
(PACK: 2 DZ.)

GROUP A/EOD
$15.00 DZ.
(PACK: 2 DZ.)

PAGE 1

*PIL2: This Pilgrim catalog page from the mid 1970s shows the smaller peachblow pitchers. Courtesy of the Pilgrim Glass Co.*

GROUP A—KRACKLED WINDOW PITCHER COLLECTION

**GROUP A/PLAIN**
SAME AS ABOVE, IN PLAIN, NOT KRACKLED FINISH.
$12.00 DOZEN PACK: 3 DOZEN

GROUP A/SG SANDWICH GLASS MINIATURES 4"

Replicas of early Sandwich Glass Pitchers

GROUP A/SG
$12.00 DZ.
PACK: 3 DOZEN ASSORTED

WINDOW
PITCHER COLLECTION
ASSORTED SHAPES,
ASSORTED COLORS
**GROUP A**
$12.00 DZ.
PACK: 3 DOZEN

# PILGRIM MINIATURES

Pilgrim Glass Miniatures make decorative window pieces, adding a touch of warmth and color to the home. Pilgrim Miniatures are best sellers everywhere. Feature them for fast turn-over and profits. AMERICA'S MOST POPULAR COLLECTION!

SPECIAL PRICE BREAK: MAKE YOUR OWN COMBINATION ORDER OF 12 DZ. OR MORE OF ANY OF GROUPS A/KRACKLED, A/SG, M/SG, A/LH, A/PLAIN, AND LB AT:
**$11.40 DZ.**
(IN LOTS OF 12 DZ. OR MORE)

GROUP M/SG SANDWICH GLASS VASES 4"

GROUP M/SG
$12.00 DOZEN
PACK: 3 DOZEN ASSORTED

GROUP A/LH   Hard to find left-handed pitchers (with spout at right angle to the handle).

*PIL3: The small peachblow items were part of Pilgrim's Miniatures. Some of the shapes on these two pages also appear in peachblow, which means the shapes not shown in peachblow probably do too. Courtesy of Pilgrim Glass Co.*

**PIL5:** *The pitcher on the right is shown in peachblow in the reprint of the catalog, but the vase on the left is not. It does appear in peachblow in the catalog with a handle, however.*

**PIL6:** *This little vase, with the original Pilgrim sticker, does not appear in the catalog in peachblow, but it does in other colors.*

**PIL7:** *Another vase similar in shape to the previous one.*

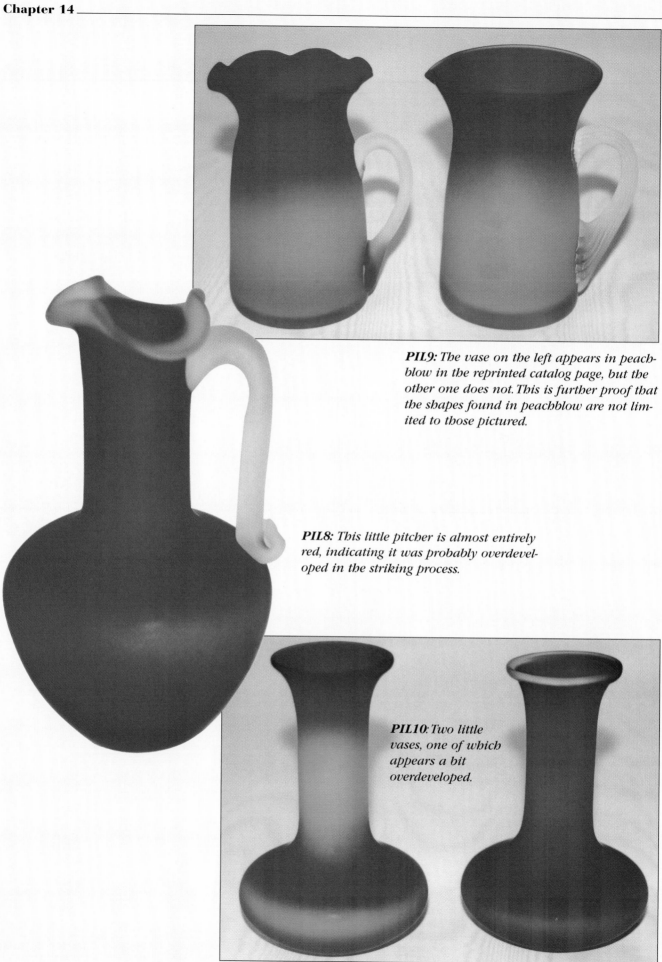

**PIL9:** *The vase on the left appears in peachblow in the reprinted catalog page, but the other one does not. This is further proof that the shapes found in peachblow are not limited to those pictured.*

**PIL8:** *This little pitcher is almost entirely red, indicating it was probably overdeveloped in the striking process.*

**PIL10:** *Two little vases, one of which appears a bit overdeveloped.*

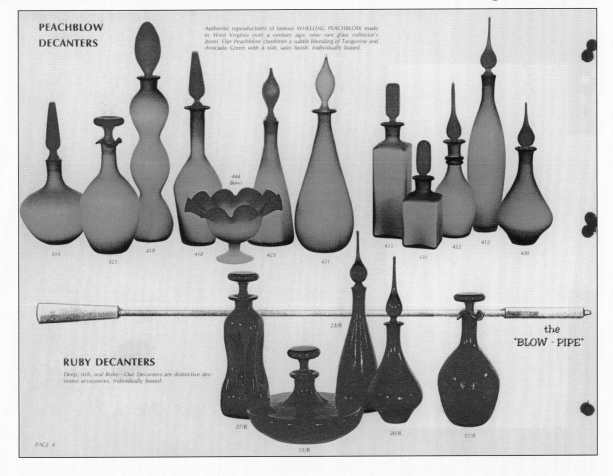

**PIL11:** *The line of large Peachblow items in the 1969 Pilgrim catalog. Courtesy of the Pilgrim Glass Co.*

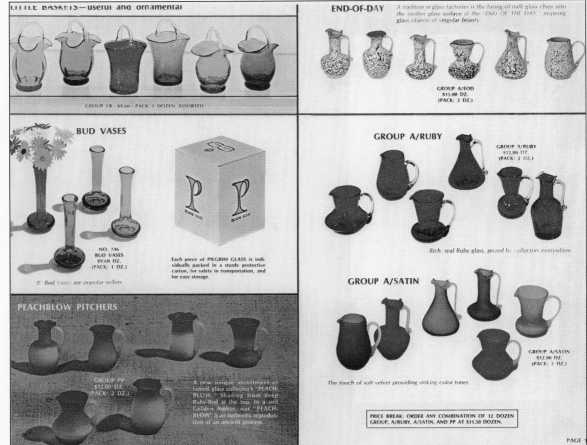

**PIL12:** *Pilgrim's assortment of Peachblow pitchers are shown in this catalog page too. Courtesy of Pilgrim Glass Co.*

*K3: The 316 PB vase, which stands 5-3/4" tall was made both with and without a handle. It's a bit easier to find without the handle, though. Authors' collection.*

# Kanawha Peachblow

The Kanawha Glass Company was located in Dunbar, West Virginia, in Kanawha County and along the Kanawha River. The company was founded in 1955 following the 1953 closing of the Dunbar Flint Glass Corp. Dunbar's general manager, D.P. Merritt, founded Kanawha.

The company initially made crystal and lighting products. By 1960, limited production of colored glass had begun. In 1974, Kanawha purchased the Shelby Earl Glass Company, a manufacturer of communion glasses. In 1988, Kanawha was sold to the Raymond Dereume Glass Company, Inc. of Punxsutawney, PA.

In 1970, Kanawha began to produce a glassware they called Peachblow. The glass was either an orangish-red going to an amber at the bottom with a white casing or a white outer layer with a red casing. The shaded Kanawha peachblow was made much the same way as Wheeling peachblow, with an amber glass over a white lining, and then partially reheated to produce the orangish-red coloring.

In 1974 Sapphire, a light blue cased over white, and Lemon, a yellow cased over white, were added to the line. Lime, a light green cased over white, was added in 1976. Only the red and the shaded cased glass colorations are consistently called "Peachblow" in catalogs. The designation PB and the Peachblow name were used as stock codes for the other colors.

In 1978 additional shapes, including a basket, appeared in the peachblow line for a total of 52 different shapes in what was apparently the line's peak. They retailed for $2 to $5 apiece.

After 1978 the number of shapes in the peachblow line decreased. The line was discontinued by 1980-1981 when the catalog featured about a dozen items, marked "discontinued." By the mid 1980s, the company offered no cased glass.

*K1: The cover of the 1970 Kanawha catalog shows the company had begun making its peachblow by that year. Courtesy of Frank M. Fenton, Fenton Art Glass Co.*

## Kanawha Peachblow Identification Card

**Proper Name:** Peachblow.

**Manufacturer:** Kanawha Glass Co., Dunbar, WV.

**Date of Production:** 1970-1981.

**Color:** Reddish orange shaded to yellow with a white interior, or white outside with a red interior casing.

**Casing:** Yes, see above.

**Finish:** Primarily glossy. A few satin pieces can occasionally be found..

**Decorations:** None.

**Special Characteristics:** No pontil marks. Although Lemon, Sapphire and Lime cased glass is not considered peachblow, they are sometime labeled "Peachblow," in addition to the PB designation, in catalogs.

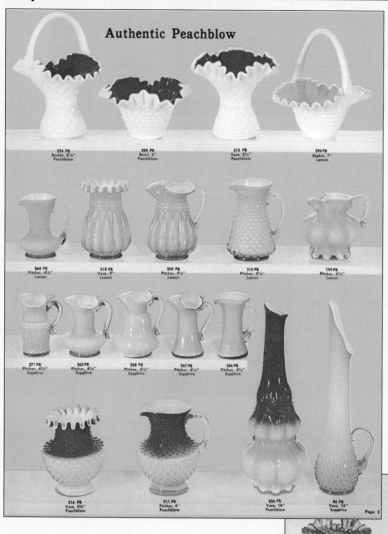

Authentic Peachblow

Page 3

*K2: This page in the 1971 catalog shows three pieces in peachblow, bottom row. The white items with the red interior casing, top row, are also referred to as "Peachblow." Note that the page is titled "Authentic Peachblow" and that all items are designated "PB" for peachblow, regardless of color. Courtesy of Frank M. Fenton, Fenton Art Glass Co.*

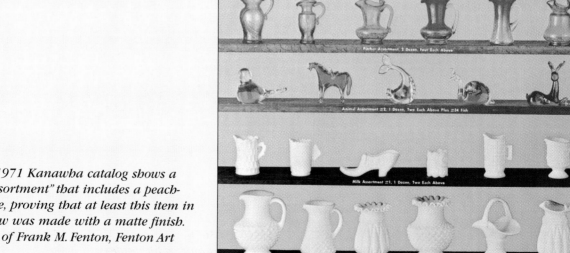

Kanawha

*K4: The 1971 Kanawha catalog shows a "satin assortment" that includes a peachblow vase, proving that at least this item in peachblow was made with a matte finish. Courtesy of Frank M. Fenton, Fenton Art Glass Co.*

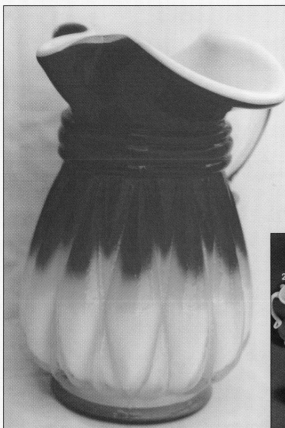

*K5: This vase, designated as 308 PB, 5-1/4" pitcher, is the same as the item shown in the 1971 catalog, only it has a handle. Authors' collection.*

*K6: Small pitchers appear in the 1976 Kanawha catalog. The six pieces in the top right hand corner of this page are designated as the "Peachblow assortment." Courtesy of Frank M. Fenton, Fenton Art Glass Co.*

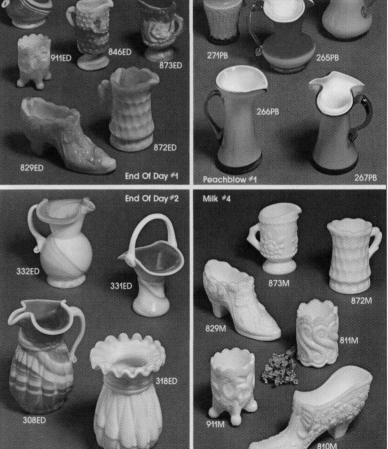

*K7: This is the 256PB piece shown in the 1976 catalog, but its coloring is quite a bit weaker.*

**K8:** *The 264PB 4-1/4" pitcher in the peachblow color. Authors' collection.*

**K9:** *The 267PB 4-1/4" pitcher in peachblow with the original company sticker. Authors' collection.*

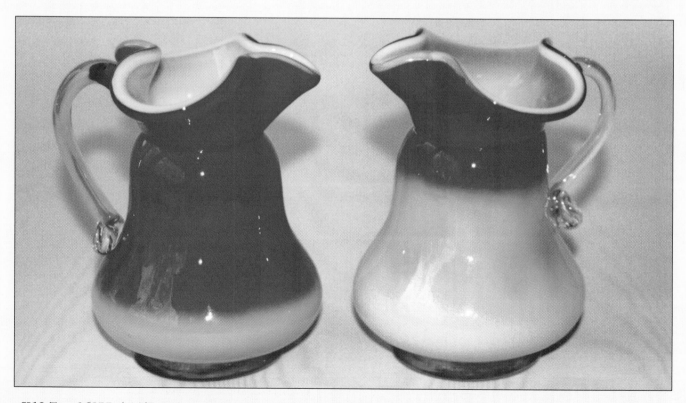

**K10:** *Two 268PB 4-1/4" pitchers. Notice the difference in color.*

***K11:*** *This page from the 1976 Kanawha catalog clearly shows that the white glass with the red interior was also considered peachblow. The white items with the Lime interior were not referred to as peachblow, but are still given the PB designation. Courtesy of Frank M. Fenton, Fenton Art Glass Co.*

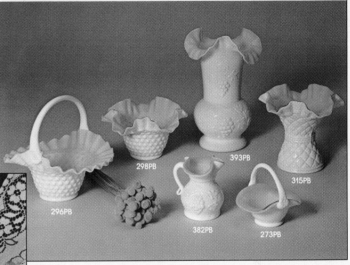

***K12:*** *Another 1976 Kanawha catalog page showing Lime and Lemon items designated "PB." Courtesy of Frank M. Fenton, Fenton Art Glass Co.*

*K13: This page from the Kanawha 1977 catalog supplement shows a few more shapes in Lime and Lemon. Since they're designated PB, they are probably also made in peachblow. Courtesy of Frank M. Fenton, Fenton Art Glass Co.*

*K14: The 432PB 6-1/2"
Toby Milk Pitcher
appears in the 1977 cata-
log supplement. Here it is
in Peachblow. A Dutch
Girl pitcher was also
made. Authors' collection.*

*K15: The 430 PB 7" pitcher
in peachblow. Authors' collection.*

*INT2: This creamer is signed
"Intaglio Designs, Ltd."*

# CHAPTER 16

# Intaglio Peachblow

Gary W. Levi, who had been affiliated with Levay, founded Intaglio, a company in Wood River, IL, that in ads is sometimes called Intaglio Glass Studio or Intaglio Design Ltd. Ads for the venture appear in Glass Collector's Digest starting in 1993 and 1994. Intaglio made a wide variety of art glass, including a line called Mimosa—"More commonly known as Peachblow" say ads, run in the December/January 1993 and October/November 1994 editions of *Glass Collector's Digest*.

"INTAGLIO'S Studio with its many gifted artisans, under the personal supervision of Gary W. Levi (Levay), is devoted to the continuation and refinement of the glass craft. Today's product complements the achievements of the earlier years. Levi feels indebted to the skilled and prolific artists and glass companies which preceded him ... Joseph Locke, innovator of agata (sic) glass, at the New England Glass Co.; Mt. Washington Peachblow from Gundersen Glass Co., later Pairpoint Glass Co.; Peachblow from the New England Glassworks; and Rosalene from Fenton," the ads says.

Intaglio made peachblow for five or six years. The ad shows 12 shapes but others were made. The shapes listed in the ad, which introduced the line, are as follows:

Three crimped rose bowl, 3" tall
Swirled paperweight, 2" diameter
Large strawberry, 3-1/2" long
Small strawberry, 2-1/2" long
Large apple, 3-1/2" tall
Small apple, 2-1/2" tall
Large ornament, 4" diameter
Small ornament, 3" diameter
Diamond ornament (diamond quilted pattern on a glass ball), 3" diameter
Basket, 6" tall
Lily vase, 4-1/2" tall (jack-in-the-pulpit shape). This is the only item in the ad noted to come in both glossy and matte finishes.

*INT1: The swirled paperweight, which appears in company ads. It is signed in script "Intaglio 1994."*

*INT3: This Intaglio piece imitates shapes found in peachblow by Mt. Washington and Fenton.*

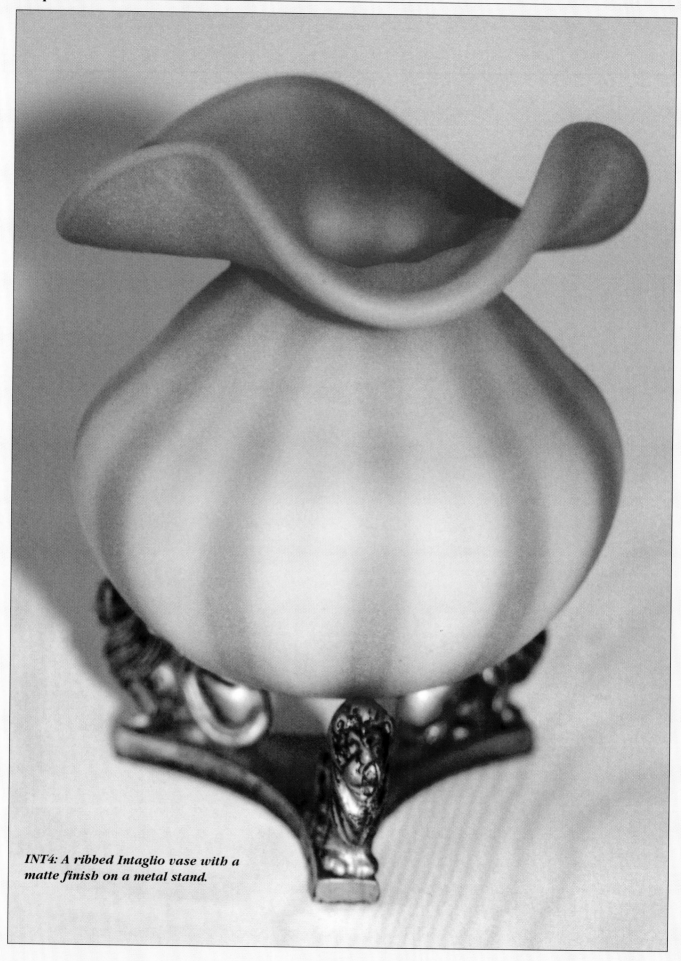

*INT4: A ribbed Intaglio vase with a matte finish on a metal stand.*

## INTAGLIO Studio Art Glass

**M**imosa - INTAGLIO's Studio with its many gifted artisans, under the personal supervision of Gary W. Levi (Levay), is devoted to the continuation and refinement of the glass craft. Today's product complements the achievements of the earlier years. Levi feels indebted to the skilled and prolific artists and glass companies which preceded him . . . Joseph Locke, innovator of agata glass, at the New England Glass Co.; Mt. Washington Peachblow from Gunderson Glass Co., later Pairpoint Glass Co.; Peachblow from the New England Glassworks; and Rosalene from Fenton.

***INT5:*** *The Intaglio ad for Mimosa/Peachblow, which ran in* Glass Collector's Digest.

### Intaglio Peachblow Identification Card

**Proper Name:** Mimosa "More commonly known as Peachblow."
**Manufacturer:** Intaglio, Wood River, IL. The company also went by Intaglio, Intaglio Designs, Ltd. and Intaglio Glass Studio.
**Date of Production:** 1993-94. Other dates possible.
**Color:** Shades from pink to white.
**Casing:** None.
**Finish:** Primarily matte. Company ads show only the lily vase in both matte and glossy finishes, although other shapes not shown in the ad are found in glossy.
**Decorations:** None.
**Special Characteristics:** Pieces are often signed in script "Intaglio" and dated. They may also be marked in other ways. The ad shows a circle with the word INTAGLIO in an arc with "Anton" written straight across at the bottom.

**MM2:** *This apple, signed Gibson, is not peachblow. Gibson made it using Blue Burmese cullet, and does not use the term "peachblow" to describe the glass produced from that cullet or any other glass in its line, past or present.*

# CHAPTER 17

# Mistakes, Misconceptions and Misunderstandings

Peachblow is one of the most confusing and misunderstood types of art glass. No matter how many times we have explained to collectors what peachblow is, we invariably are presented with a piece of glass or a photo of it and asked if it is peachblow. The vast majority of the time, the piece is not. It seems that an explanation of what is not peachblow is just as important as a discussion of what it is. This chapter is an attempt to cover the myriad of glass types commonly mistaken for peachblow, along with an explanation of why they are not peachblow.

## Fenton Blue Burmese

We decided to start out with this one because it represents a bit of a gray area. Fenton does not call it peachblow, but Blue Burmese. Still, one cannot help but notice that the dusty rose to dusty blue shading resembles Mt. Washington peachblow. So does that make it peachblow?

It's apparently made with a formula similar to what was used for Mt. Washington peachblow, but because the company does not call it such, we believe it is not truly peachblow. As stated in the introduction, peachblow is really a name applied to a line of glass, rather than a description of a particular type of glass. Peachblow varies from company to company. One particular formula or look is not the key that makes a line peachblow, the way it is for Burmese. The key is the company nomenclature.

If we say Blue Burmese is peachblow, even when the company didn't call it that, we open the door for all kinds of things, from Rosalene to even Burmese, to be called peachblow. We believe that would be imprecise and misleading.

## Gibson Peachblow?

If Fenton Blue Burmese is not peachblow, then neither is the shaded pink to blue-gray line by Gibson. We were told by a factory representative that Gibson buys Blue Burmese cullet to produce what collectors might term peachblow. But Gibson doesn't call it peachblow.

## Webb Cased Pink Glass

We made the argument that Webb Peach Glass has a peach hue, therefore the shaded pink to lighter pink or

***MM1***: *A lovely piece of decorated Fenton Blue Burmese, which the company is currently producing. It looks very similar to Mt. Washington peachblow, but the company doesn't call it peachblow. Collection of Louis O. St. Aubin, Jr.*

pink to white glass commonly identified as Webb peachblow is not. Many times these pieces are indeed Webb, but not Webb peachblow.

## Pink Cased Glass By Other Firms

Naturally, Webb isn't the only firm to make pink cased glass. But, these items are not peachblow, unless we can prove that the makers called them peachblow. It's well known that various companies in the US and abroad made pink cased glass without any attempt to sell it as peachblow. Remember not everything with a pink or even a peach hue is peachblow. In fact, it's more likely to not be!

*MM3: This Webb vase with Jules Barbe decoration shades from rich rose pink to white. Therefore, it's not Webb peachblow, but pink cased glass. Photo by Bill Pitt, courtesy of Brookside Antiques.*

## Pink Satin Glass

Take a piece of pink cased glass and give it a bath in hydrofluoric acid and you have pink satin glass. But this is no more peachblow than glossy cased pink glass is. We know companies made satin glass and marketed it as satin glass, so it was not ever really considered to be peachblow.

## Joseph Webb Peachbloom?

Opaque glass shading from deep rose pink to lighter pink and with a white interior has been found with Phoenix Glass Co. paper labels. It's thought that this glass was produced while Joseph Webb worked at Phoenix developing art glass. However, we have no evidence that this glassware was actually called "peachbloom" by the company.

## Harrach Peachblow?

The Bohemian firm of Harrach produced a line of shaded cased glass which is similar to both Webb peachblow and the pink cased glass commonly mistaken for Webb peachblow. In fact, this glassware is often found decorated with a gold enameling very similar to that of Webb decorator Jules Barbe. Collectors frequently refer to this glass as Harrach peachblow.

We contacted Bohemian glass writer/researchers Robert and Deborah Truitt and Gary Baldwin to get started on our research into Bohemian peachblow. What they told us was that we really need not look any further. In their work, they had not uncovered any evidence that Bohemian glassmakers used the name peachblow, in any of its various spellings, to sell their glass. That means there is no such thing as Harrach peachblow, nor is there such a thing as Bohemian peachblow in general.

*MM4: Subtle colorations are difficult to capture in photos. This photo, shows the difference between pink cased glass and peach colored glass. The vase on the left is Webb, the peachy one on the right is Stevens & Williams, and possibly their Peach Bloom. It's not the same company, granted, but the photo still captures the difference in coloration that distinguishes peachblow from pink glass.*

The Truitts did point out that Bohemian glassmakers exported their products all over the world. And, it's quite possible that an independent importer capitalized in the popularity of the term and referred to Bohemian glass as peachblow. We know that L. Strauss & Sons, wholesale distributors of imported glass and china, imported pottery facsimiles of the Morgan vase believed to have been made in Bohemia. And in our research, we have come across photos of glass bottle-shaped vases imitating the famous vase, though they were not shaded. So it's quite possible that Strauss or other importers used the name peachblow for shaded pink or peach cased glass. However, our research in this country did not uncover any direct evidence.

So, at this time, we have to say that peachblow is not the correct term to describe the line of Harrach glass in question. Nor is it accurately applied to any other Bohemian glass, at least not without further proof.

One way to prove the so-called Harrach peachblow is not peachblow is by the so-called "propeller mark" sometimes found on it. For years, it was believed the propeller mark was a Webb mark. However, it has since been proven that this not a Webb mark, but the Harrach family crest. The mark is found on pieces that are Harrach, and not Webb. There's no evidence to suggest that Harrach called this glass peachblow, so it's not peachblow.

We've been able to examine pieces of Webb peachblow and the Harrach line side by side. Harrach pontils are polished, but show only the outside layer of glass. Frequently, Webb pontils, which are also polished, show a cross section of the different layers of glass. In addition, the Harrach glass is quite a bit heavier than Webb items, whether they're peachblow or not. The red hue on the Harrach pieces is also considerably darker than those found on Webb pieces, whether they're peachblow or cased pink glass. These clues should aid the person trying to determine if an unmarked piece is Harrach or Webb.

## Burmese

Burmese is mistaken for peachblow more often than any other type of glass with the possible exception of pink cased or satin glass. But with Burmese, the line is crystal clear. Burmese is not peachblow, not ever.

Burmese is a single-layered semi-opaque heat sensitive glass which shades from a rose pink to salmon yellow. Burmese was first patented in 1885 by Frederick Shirley, as discussed in Chapter 4. It was then produced by Thomas Webb and Sons in England, by the Italians in the 1960s, and then by Fenton starting in the 1970s. Gibson has also begun producing a line of Burmese and other companies are likely to follow. Burmese always has the same basic pink to yellow color shading no matter how old it is or who made it. One may be brighter than another, some pieces are decorated while others are not. But all Burmese is simply Burmese. It is not peachblow in any way, shape or form. Nor is there a such thing as "Burmese Peachblow." It's either Burmese or it's peachblow. It can't be both.

*MM5: A shaded pink to white cased glass vase of unknown origin. Photo courtesy Fred Wishnie, Wishful Things.*

*MM6: A shaded pink to white pear. It's unknown if it's cased, since we can't see inside it. It may be Webb, but even if it is, the peach hue is not there, making it not peachblow.*

*MM7: This lovely bride's bowl is shaded pink to white. In the absence of an attribution and evidence that the maker called it peachblow, we must conclude it's not peachblow. Photo courtesy of Angie Hudock.*

*MM8: This lovely footed rose bowl is probably Stevens & Williams Mat-su-no-ke, judging by the style of the applied crystal flowers. However, it shades from pink to white, making it not an example of peachblow. Collection of Stu Horn.*

## New Martinsville Peachblow?

The New Martinsville Glass Mfg. Co. produced a line of glassware which consists of an outer layer of gold, cased with a layer of pink, which creates an iridescent appearance. This line was originally called Muranese. However, it is frequently called "peachblow," a misnomer which began with enterprising antique dealers in the 1940s, long after production of the line had ceased in 1907.

## Sandwich Peachblow?

A line of glass in a strawberry ice cream pink, often with frosted clear applied edging or feet, was for years called "Sandwich peachblow." However, no evidence exists to suggest that Boston & Sandwich produced anything called peachblow. Even the true origin of the so-called "Sandwich peachblow" items are in doubt. Current thinking is that this glass was made in England or Bohemia.

## Agata

We mention Agata in Chapter 5, but mention it again here to emphasize that it is not peachblow. New England took Wild Rose, which was their peachblow, and added a stain, resulting in an effect that looks like oil floating on water. They called this Agata.

Agata is noteworthy because New England made facsimiles of the Morgan vase in this line, and these look more like the real Morgan vase than any line of peachblow!

## Plated Amberina And Wheeling Drape

If we're going to mention Agata, it makes sense to

cover Plated Amberina and the so-called "Wheeling Drape."

Plated Amberina is a New England line which looks remarkably similar to Wheeling peachblow. The primary difference is the ribbing found in Plated Amberina and not in Wheeling peachblow. The linings of Plated Amberina pieces also tend to have an opalescence not found in the Wheeling line.

Wheeling Drape has the same basic coloring as Plated Amberina but has a draped pattern in the glass. Many theories abound but its exact origin is unknown. Incidentally, this cased drape pattern is found in other colors such as pink.

The Italians reproduced Plated Amberina in the 1960s and 1970s, just as they did many lines of Victorian art glass. The Italian versions are quite heavy, have rough pontil marks, and thick stark white interior linings. Any crimps a piece may have are typically uneven, and the piece may even be lopsided, a characteristic you won't find in authentic pieces.

## Anything Else?

Peachblow has many faces, but that doesn't mean it's everywhere. The peachblow lines discussed in this book are the only ones known. If it's not one of them, it's not peachblow.

We've made every attempt to be as thorough as possible, especially with the Victorian lines, which are the most expensive. If you have a piece which you believe to be Victorian, but it doesn't appear in the first five chapters, our advice is to proceed with caution. Yours may be a Victorian piece, and it may even be a quality piece. But that doesn't make it peachblow. Knowing that will no doubt prevent many costly mistakes.

*MM9: A pink cased glass cruet which shows no sign of a peach hue cannot be considered peachblow since we don't know who made it and therefore, have no idea whether the maker considered it peachblow.*

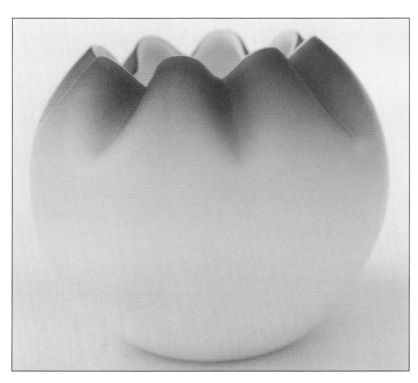

*MM10: As avid collectors of rose bowls, we're often asked by fellow collectors if a piece such as this is peachblow. It's not peachblow by any stretch of the imagination! It's pink satin glass. Authors' collection.*

*MM12: Lovely though it is, this perfume is not peachblow.*

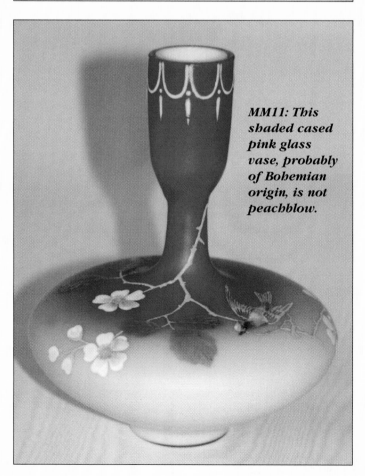

*MM11: This shaded cased pink glass vase, probably of Bohemian origin, is not peachblow.*

*MM13: This decorated ewer is another example of pink satin glass, not peachblow. The Severn Collection.*

*MM14: Mother-of-Pearl satin glass, in which air is trapped between layers of glass, is not mistaken for peachblow as often as other types of glass. But we include these examples to aid those who may confuse the two, particularly if the Mother-of-Pearl is pink. The Severn Collection.*

*MM15: A marked Harrach rose bowl shown alongside a Webb peachblow punch cup. Note the differences in color. The Harrach piece is definitely darker and what shading it has is minimal, especially compared to the Webb piece. The Severn Collection.*

*MM16: The bottoms of the two pieces. Note how the pontil on the Webb punch cup shows not only the outer layer of glass, but the casing too. The Harrach piece has a polished pontil but you cannot see the inside layer of glass. Also, note the Harrach mark.*

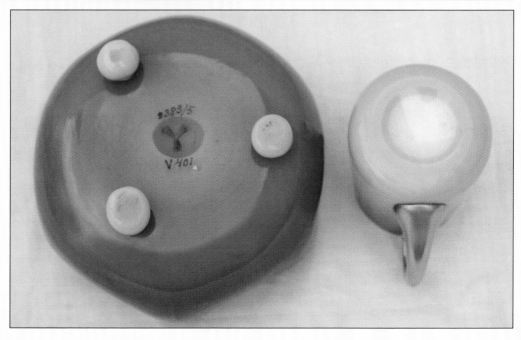

**MM17:** *The similarities in the decoration can be seen between the Harrach rose bowl, left, and the Webb peachblow rose bowl, right, from the authors' collection.*

**MM18:** *A close up of the Harrach decoration. It is not as raised as the Webb version, and is outlined in white. Webb decorations are not outlined this way.*

**MM19:** *Another piece, believed to be Harrach. This one is more shaded than the rose bowl shown in the previous photos. Nevertheless, it's not peachblow because it's Harrach. Photo courtesy of Angie Hudock.*

**MM20:** *You can see the mark on the bottom of this piece. Some of the interior casing is visible but the pontil is still considerably different than that of a piece of Webb.*

*MM22: The mark on the piece in the photo at right.*

*MM21: This one wouldn't be peach-blow on any account. Even if it were Webb, it shades from darker pink to lighter pink, and has no peach hue. But the piece is Harrach, ending any debate. The Severn Collection.*

*MM23: These cased plates appear to be Harrach, due to the dark, unshaded red on the one side and the decorative style, which is similar to marked pieces shown here. However, we did not handle the pieces, so we can only speculate at best. In any event, they are clearly not American, and even if they were Webb, they are missing the peach hue necessary to call them peachblow. Photo courtesy of Angie Hudock.*

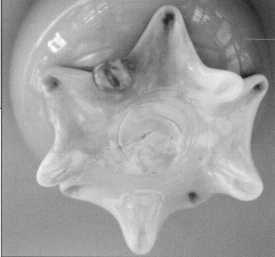

*MM24: This rose bowl was identified as Webb peachblow by a reputable seller. However, having handled it in person, we don't believe it's Webb. It's far too heavy for one thing. For another, the foot is made of one piece of glass, a style more typical of Bohemian makers than English ones. And lastly, the color is not quite right. The bottom color is more of a dirty white than is typically found on Webb. Perhaps it's Harrach. Perhaps not. In any event, it's not peachblow. Collection of Stu Horn.*

*MM25: The bottom of the bowl shown in the previous photo.*

*MM26: Pink to yellow coloring may leave you thinking "peach," but it's not peachblow. It's Burmese. Photo courtesy of Stu Horn.*

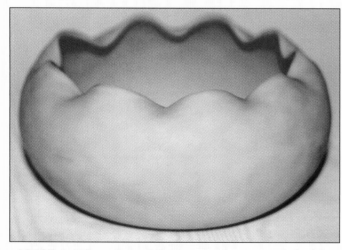

*MM27: Another piece of Burmese, this one made by Mt. Washington. Again, it's not peachblow. Authors' collection.*

*MM28: No type of Burmese is more commonly mistaken for peachblow than that produced in Italy during the 1960s and 1970s. This tumbler has the same band of purple sometimes found on Italian reproductions of Mt. Washington peachblow. But its pink to yellow coloration is clearly that of Burmese, not peachblow.*

**MM29:** *A 1960s Italian rose bowl with its original stickers. The oval red sticker identifies the origin of the piece. The blue and white sticker identifies the importer, Koscherak Brothers, Inc., of New York, NY.*

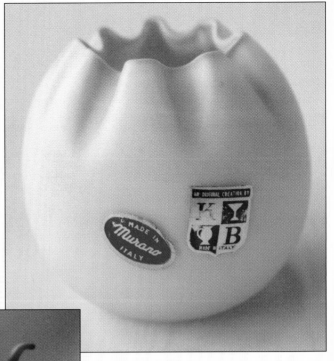

**MM30:** *This is another example of 1960s Italian Burmese. The pink is rather dark and the yellow unusually pale. But it is Burmese. This shape, or similar ones may be found in Italian peachblow. Either way, Italian pieces like this are commonly mistaken for Stevens & Williams because of the applied flowers and feet.*

**MM31:** *The berry prunt on the bottom of the Italian piece.*

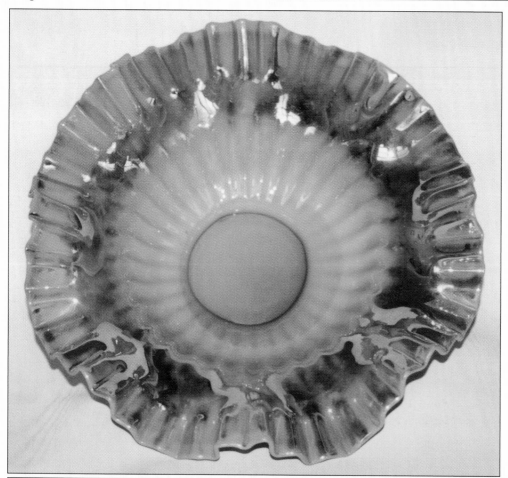

*MM32: The interior of the New Martinsville Muranese bowl. Reference materials on the line say the exterior layer of glass was gold, which gave it an iridescent affect. The item is on display at the Fenton factory museum and was photographed courtesy of Frank M. Fenton, Fenton Art Glass Co.*

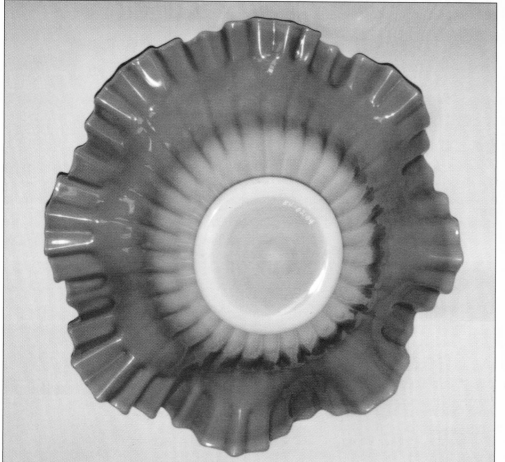

*MM33: The outer pink layer of glass on the Muranese bowl.*

*MM34: A so-called "Sandwich peachblow" vase. Boston & Sandwich did not make a line called peachblow, however. The true origin of these pieces is unknown. Collection of Stu Horn.*

*MM36: An Agata rendition of the Morgan vase, c. 1887. It would seem likely that the vase was also made in New England peachblow, but so far, none have surfaced.*

*MM35: Agata, made by the New England Glass Works, is a variation of peachblow, since the company added a metallic stain to their Wild Rose line, which was their peachblow. However, the company did not call this line peachblow, and collectors generally don't either. Photo by Bill Pitt, courtesy of Brookside Antiques.*

**MM38:** *So called "Wheeling Drape" also has coloration similar to that found in Wheeling peachblow. The colors are a bit lighter, however, and of course the drape pattern is the dead giveaway that this is not peachblow.*

**MM37:** *This piece of Plated Amberina is a bit overdeveloped, resulting in darker than usual shading. Still, you can see that the colors are basically the same as those found in Wheeling peachblow. Plated Amberina is not peachblow, however. Photo by Bill Pitt, courtesy of Brookside Antiques.*

**MM39:** *A 1960s Italian copy of Plated Amberina. Note the thick interior lining and uneven crimping. Still, the colors are quite lovely. Just be sure you don't mistake it for the real thing. Rose bowls are not known to have been made in Plated Amberina. Authors' collection.*

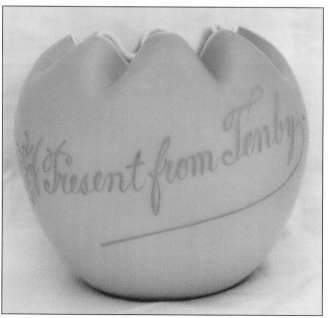

**MM40:** *It's peachy, but it's not peachblow! It's apricot satin glass. Authors' collection.*

# Bibliography

## Books

Bredehoft, Neila & Tom. *Hobbs, Brockunier & Co. Glass Identification and Value Guide.* Collector Books, Paducah, KY. 1997.

Bushell, S.W. *Oriental Ceramic Art.* Crown Publishers, Inc., New York. 1980.

Dimitroff, Thomas P. *Frederick Carder and His Steuben Glass.* Schiffer Publishing, Atglen, PA. 1998.

Fauster, Carl U. *Libbey Glass Since 1818.* Len Beach Press, Toledo, OH. 1979.

Hajdamach, Charles R. *British Glass: 1800-1914.* Antique Collectors' Club. Ltd. Woodbridge, England. 1991.

Heacock, William. *Fenton Glass The First Twenty-Five Years.* Antique Publications, Marietta, OH. 1978.

Heacock, William. *Fenton Glass The Second Twenty-Five Years.* Antique Publications, Marietta, OH. 1980.

Lechner, Mildred & Ralph. *The World of Salt Shakers.* Collector Books, Paducah, KY. 1992.

Lee, Ruth Webb. *Nineteenth-Century Art Glass.* Barrows & Co., New York, NY. 1966.

Manley, Cyril. *Decorative Victorian Glass.* Van Nostrand Reinhold Company, NY, NY. 1981.

Measell, James and W.C. "Red" Rotteis. *The L.G. Wright Glass Company.* Antique Publications, Marietta, OH. 1997.

Miller, Everett R. & Addie R. *The New Martinsville Glass Story.* Richardson Publishing, Marietta, OH. 1972.

National Imperial Glass Collector's Society and edited by James Measell. *Imperial Glass Encyclopedia Vol. III.* Antique Publications, Marietta, OH. 1999.

Pina, Leslie. *Fifties Glass.* Schiffer Publishing, Atglen, PA. 1993.

Pina, Leslie. *Circa Fifties Glass.* Schiffer Publishing, Atglen, PA. 1997.

Revi, Albert Christian. *American Art Nouveau Glass.* Schiffer Publishing, Exton, PA. 1968.

Revi, Albert Christian. *Nineteenth-Century Art Glass: Its Genesis and Development.* Schiffer Publishing, Exton, PA. 1967.

Shuman, John A. III. *The Collector's Encyclopedia of American Art Glass.* Collector Books, Paducah, KY. 1991.

Woodward, Hiram W., Jr. *Asian Art in the Walters Art Gallery.* Baltimore, MD. 1991.

Woodward, H.W. *Art, Feat and Mystery: The Story of Thomas Webb & Sons, Glassmakers.* Mark & Moody Limited, Sturbridge, England. 1978.

## Periodicals

Anonymous. "The Eight Prescribed Peachbloom Shapes Bearing K'ang Hsi Marks." *Oriental Art,* Winter 1957.

Gaines, Edith. "Peachblow Glass." *Art & Antiques,* September-October 1982.

Kerr, Rose. "The William T. Walters Collection of Qing Dynasty Porcelain." *Orientations,* April 1991.

Kilbourne, Joan. "The Magic of Peachblow." *Glass Review,* January 1988.

Revi, Albert Christian. "American Shaded Wares of the Late 19th Century." *Hobbies,* January 1956.

Revi, Albert Christian. "Mrs. Morgan's Peach Bloom Vase and Its Facsimiles in Glass and Pottery," *The Spinning Wheel,* January-February 1965.

Revi, Albert C. "Who Remembers Peachblow?" *Crockery & Glass Journal,* November 1957.

Rice, Ferill J. "Fenton's Peach Blow, Peach Crest and Black Rose." *Glass Collector's Digest,* February/March 1990.

Six, Dean. "Kanawha Peachblow," *Glass Collector's Digest,* October/November 1992.

Wintermute, H. Ogden. "Wheeling Peach Blow and Rainbow Mother of Pearl Satin." Unknown. January 1962.

# Price Guide

Since we don't collect peachblow, frankly we're not all that in touch with the market. (On the light side, no one can accuse us of setting prices to our own advantage!) That didn't solve the problem of accurate pricing information, however.

To be blunt, we had lots of help. Louis O. St. Aubin, Jr. of Brookside Antiques helped us with prices on the Webb, Wheeling, Mt. Washington, New England, World's Fair, Gundersen and Pairpoint peachblow. The National Imperial Glass Collectors Society helped us with the prices for Imperial.

For the other types, we gathered data at shows and other events, (we attended the liquidation sales for the L.G. Wright Glass Co., for example) and we perused other price guides for the opinions of other authors.

Although we sometimes wonder if anyone reads these price guide introductions, we feel obligated to point out that these figures are to be used only as a guide. Many things influence pricing, including geography, the condition of the item and buyer taste. The prices quoted here are retail prices and are generally toward the high end of what you'd expect to pay. They're certainly not a guarantee that your item is worth what is stated here.

Some items are not priced due to lack of data. Either the item is too rare to price, or, too new to appear on the secondary market with any frequency. We'd rather not price it than to make up a figure. To make the guide easier to use, we have included unpriced pieces, marked "no price," so that you know these items weren't omitted from the guide by mistake.

## Chapter 2: Webb Peachblow

| | |
|---|---|
| Vase (WE1) | $750-$950 |
| Small vase (WE2) | $750-$950 |
| Punch cup (WE3) | $200-$300 |
| Rose bowls | |
| Decorated (WE5) | $500-$750 |
| Undecorated (WE4, WE5) | $400-$600 |
| Vases, Jules Barbe enameling (WE8) | $750-$950 ea. |
| Rose bowl, 3 toes (WE9) | $400-$600 |
| Plate, Jules Barbe decoration (WE10) | $400-$600 |
| Cracker jar, Jules Barbe enameling (WE11) | $1,500-$2,000 |
| Vase, Jules Barbe decoration (WE12) | $400-$550 |
| Vase, dragon decoration (WE13) | $750-$950 |
| Mini egg-shaped rose bowl (WE14) | $450-$650 |
| Mini vase, amber foot (WE15) | $400-$600 |

## Stevens & Williams Peachblow

| | |
|---|---|
| Vase (S&W1) | $750-$900 |
| Rose bowl (S&W3) | $200-$300 |

## Carder/Steuben Peachblow

| | |
|---|---|
| Vase/lamp base | no price |

## Chapter 3: Wheeling Peachblow

| | |
|---|---|
| Morgan vase (WH1) | |
| Without stand | $750-$1,000 |
| With stand | $1,500-$2,000 |
| Witch's ball (WH2) | no price |
| Jack-in-the-pulpit, purple lining (WH3) | no price |
| Lamp (WH4) | $8,000-$10,000 |
| Spangled peachblow ewers (WH5) | no price |
| Vases | |
| Large ovoid vase (WH6) | $3,000-$4,000 |
| No. 6 vase (WH7, WH8) | $1,500-$2,000 |
| Double gourd, No. 7 vase (WH9, WH10) | $2,000-$2,500 |
| No. 11 vase (WH11 left, WH16 left) | $750-$900 |
| No. 12 vase (WH12) | $750-$900 |
| No. 13 vase (WH13) | $1,250 |
| No. 13 vase small (WH14) | $600-$800 |
| No. 14 vase (WH15, WH16 right) | $750-$900 |
| No. 21 vase (WH17) | $3,500-$4,500 |
| Jugs and bottles | |
| Claret jug, No. 322 (WH18, WH19) | $2,000-$2,500 |
| Water bottle, No. 3 (WH20) | $900-$1,200 |
| Pelican jug, No. 324 (WH21) | $2,500-$3,500 |
| Stove pip tankard #321 (WH22) | $4,000-$6,000 |
| Tankard 91-7 (WH23, WH24) | $3,500-$4,500 |
| Jug 319 (WH25, WH26) | $2,000-$3,000 |
| No. 319 jug, no handle (WH27) | $1,500-$2,500 |
| Cruets and decanters | |
| Ball cruet (WH28) | $2,000-$2,500 |
| No. 4 Pilgrim decanter (WH29) | $2,000-$3,000 |
| No. 308 oil (WH30) | $1,200-$1,500 |
| No. 312 oil (WH31) | $1,000-$1,500 |
| No. 1 spooner (WH32) | $500-$750 |
| No. 1 creamer (WH33) | $600-$800 |
| No. 1 sugar (WH34) | $600-$800 |
| No. 1 butter (WH35) | $600-$800 |
| No. 1 sugar and creamer in silver (WH36) | $1,500-$2,000 |
| No. 2 finger bowl (WH37, WH38) | $600-$800 |
| Vases (No. 5, No. 4, No. 2, No. 1, No. 0 (WH39, WH40) | $750-$950 |
| No. 93 finger bowl (WH42) | $400-$600 |
| No. 97 Molasses can (WH43) | $2,500-$3,000 |
| No. 226 salt pepper mustard in silver holder (WH44) | $2,000-$2,500 |
| No. 226 mustard pot, alone (WH45) | $500-$750 |

| | |
|---|---|
| No. 236 tumbler (WH46, WH47) | $450-$500 |
| No. 314 celery (WH48 left) | $750-$900 |
| No. 314 spooner (WH48 right) | $650-$750 |
| No. 507 Custard (WH49) | $450-$500 |
| Sugar Sifter (WH50) | $1,200-$1,500 |
| Pear (WH52, WH51) | $600-$800 |
| Apple (WH53) | $600-$800 |

## Chapter 4: Mt. Washington Peachblow

| | |
|---|---|
| Gourd vase | |
|     Undecorated (MW3) | $2,500-$3,000 |
|     Decorated (MW3) | $4,000-$5,000 |
|     Decorated, Queen's design (MW1) | $9,500 + |
| Gourd vase, slender (MW5) | $4,000-$6,000 |
| Double gourd (MW6) | |
|     Undecorated | $2,500-$3,000 |
|     Decorated | $3,500-$4,000 |
| Corset vase, decorated (MW7) | $7,500-$9,500 |
| Footed bowl, large (MW8) | $5,000-$7,500 |
| Footed bowl (MW9) | $4,000-$5,000 |
| Pouch vase (MW10) | $6,000-$6,500 |
| Hat shaped ruffled bowl (MW11) | $3,500-$4,500 |
| Bowl, applied peachblow rim (MW12) | $5,000-$6,000 |
| Lily vase (MW13) | $2,500-$3,000 |
| Frilly lily (MW15 left) | no price |
| Crimped jack-in-the-pulpit, 13" | |
|     (MW15 right) | $4,000-$6,000 |
| Small crimped jack-in-the-pulpit (MW16) | $3,000-$4,000 |
| Small crimped jack-in-the-pulpit, decorated | |
|     (MW17) | $4,000-$5,000 |
| Vase, from cruet mold (MW18) | $3,000-$4,000 |
| Cruet, undecorated (MW19) | $4,000-$5,000 |
| Cruet, decorated (MW20) | $7,500-$9,500 |
| Oil bottle (MW21) | $1,500-$2,000 |
| Salt shaker, ribbed (MW22) | $1,000-$1,500 |
| Creamer and sugar set (MW23) | $5,000-$6,000 |
| Wishbone sugar bowl, rare decoration | |
|     (MW24) | $5,000-$6,000 |
| Sugar bowl, decorated (MW25) | $3,000-$3,500 |
| Creamer (MW26) | $2,000-$3,000 |
| Creamer, petticoat style, ruffled top | |
|     (MW27) | $2,500-$3,000 |
| Bulbous pitcher, undecorated (MW28) | $3,500-$4,000 |
| Bulbous pitcher, decorated (MW29) | $7,500-$8,500 |
| Finger bowl (MW30) | $2,000-$2,500 |
| Tankard (MW31, left) | $6,000-$7,500 |
| Bulbous pitcher (MW31, right) | $6,000-$7,500 |
| Pedestal pitcher (MW32) | $4,000-$6,000 |
| Finger/shallow rose bowl, decorated | |
|     (MW33) | $3,500-$4,000 |
| Rose bowl, outward turned crimps (MW34) | $2,000-$2,500 |
| Tricornered bowl (MW35) | $1,500-$2,000 |
| Pickle castor, pickle castor insert (MW36, MW37) | no price |
| Hobnail cream pitcher (MW38) | no price |
| Square top toothpick, decorated (MW39) | $3,500-$4,000 |
| Bulbous, square top toothpick (MW40) | $2,500-$3,000 |
| Tricorner toothpick (MW40) | $2,500-$3,000 |
| Demitasse cup/saucer set (MW41) | $3,500-$4,000 |

| | |
|---|---|
| Ruffled plate, small, decorated (MW42) | $300-$400 |
| Tumbler (MW43) | $1,000-$1,500 |
| Whiskey taster (MW43) | $1,000-$1,500 |
| Undeveloped | |
|     Ostrich egg perfume, decorated | |
|       (MW44) | $1,500-$2,000 |
|     Egg salts, decorated (MW45, MW46) | $250-$350 each |
|     Egg sugar shakers, decorated | |
|       (MW47, MW48) | $1,000-$1,500 |
|     Tomato salt, decorated (MW49) | $250-$350 |
|     Tomato sugar shaker, decorated | |
|       (MW50) | $1,500-$2,000 |

## Chapter 5: New England Peachblow

| | |
|---|---|
| Curio vases | |
|     Petticoat (NE12) | $300-$450 |
|     Flared bottom (NE2) | $400-$500 |
|     Glossy, flared bottom (NE3) | $350-$500 |
|     Shoulder (NE4) | $400-$600 |
|     Applied rigaree (NE5) | $400-$500 |
| Jack-in-the-pulpit (NE6) | $2,000-$2,500 |
| Lily vases | |
|     6", 8" or 9" (NE7) | $750-$950 |
|     Larger (not shown) | $1,000-$1,500 |
|     Decorated (NE8) | $2,500-$3,000 |
|     In silverplate holder (NE9) | $600-$750 |
| Vases | |
|     Cup vase (NE10) | $800-$1,200 |
|     Bulbous stick vase (NE11, NE11A) | $900-$1,200 |
|     Bulbous stick vase, decorated (NE1) | $2,000-$2,500 |
|     Gourd vase (NE 13) | $750-$900 |
|     Gourd vase, narrow neck, pinched | |
|       (NE 14) | $1,500-$2,000 |
|     Gourd vase, narrow neck, decorated | |
|       (NE14) | $2,500-$3,000 |
|     Bulbous bottom, pinched, large (NE15) | $2,500-$3,500 |
|     Double gourd (NE16) | $1,000-$1,200 |
|     Flared top vase (NE17) | $750-$950 |
|     Bulbous vase, flared top | |
|       (NE18A, NE18B) | $1,000-$1,500 |
|     Enameled vase (NE19) | $1,500-$2,000 |
|     Bulbous vase, narrow rim (NE20) | $750-$950 |
|     Pouch vase, spider decoration (NE21) | $3,000-$4,000 |
|     Bottle vase (NE22, NE23) | $750-$950 |
|     Bottle vase, large, undecorated (NE24) | $1,000-$1,500 |
|     Bottle vase, large, decorated | |
|       (NE25, NE26) | $3,500-$5,000 |
|     Tricornered, ruffled (NE27) | $1,000-$1,500 |
|     Tightly ruffled top (NE28) | $1,200-$1,500 |
|     Bud vase (NE 29) | $750-$900 |
| Celery | |
|     Square, pinched (NE 31) | $600-$750 |
|     Ruffled (NE32) | $750-$1,000 |
|     Celery (NE33) | $1,000-$1,500 |
| Spooner (NE34) | $500-$700 |
| Nappy (NE35) | $750-$1,000 |

Creamer

| | | |
|---|---|---|
| Bulbous, (NE36) | | $750-$950 |
| Petticoat, trefoil (NE37) | | $1,000-$1,500 |
| Vase, without handle (NE38) | | $900-$1,200 |
Sugar and creamer set (NE39) | | $3,000-$3,500 |
Cruet (NE40) | | $1,500-$2,000 |

Pitchers

| | |
|---|---|
| Tankard (NE41) | $1,500-$2,000 |
| Milk (NE41) | $900-$1,200 |
| Square top (NE42) | |
| 4.5" | $900-$1,200 |
| 8.5" | $1,500-$2,000 |
| Milk Pitcher, ruffled top, (NE43) | no price |

Toothpick

| | |
|---|---|
| Tricorner (NE44) | $650-$750 |
| Square top, Kate Greenaway holder (NE45) | $1,000-$1,200 |

Finger bowl, ruffled top (NE46) — $400-$600

Finger bowl and underplate, ruffled (NE47) — $1,000-$1,500 set

Ruffled finger or berry (NE48, NE49) — $500-$750

Ruffled berry or ice cream bowl (NE50) — $1,500-$2,000

Large berry bowl (NE51) — $1,500-$2,000

Finger bowl, smooth top (NE52) — $600-$750

Salt shaker (NE53) — $500-$700

Salt and pepper shakers in silver holder (NE54) — $1,500-$2,000

Punch cup (NE55, NE56) — $300-$400

Whiskey taster (NE58)

| | |
|---|---|
| Decorated | $750-$1,000 |
| Undecorated | $300-$400 |

Tumbler (NE59) — $350-$500

Tumbler, fern cut (NE60) — no price

## Chapter 6: World's Fair Peachblow

Pears (WF1) — $100-$125

Pear, decorated (WF2) — $200-$300

Sock darners (WF3) — $100-$125

"Christmas ornament" (WF4) — no price

Rose bowls (WF5, WF7, WF8)

| | |
|---|---|
| Undecorated | $250-$350 |
| Decorated | $400-$500 |

Rose bowls (ribbed - WF9) — $500-$700

Jack-in-the-pulpits (WF10) — $300-$500

Jack-in-the-pulpit (WF13) — $900-$1200

Creamers

| | |
|---|---|
| Petticoat ribbed (WF11) | $400-$600 |
| Other styles | $350-$500 |
| Decorated (WF12) | $600-$750 |

Sugar and creamer set, WF logo (WF14) — $900-$1,200

Salt shaker (WF15) — no price

Rose bowl (WF16) — $450-$750

## Chapter 7: Gundersen Peachblow

Vases

| | |
|---|---|
| Urn (G1) | $500-$750 |
| Banjo (G2) | $600-$800 |
| Cornucopia (G3) | $400-$500 |
| Trumpet (G4) | $400-$500 |
| Trumpet, unusual base (G5) | $1,000-$1,500 |
| Lily vase, one piece, hollow base (G6) | $1,000-$1,500 |
| Jack-in-the-pulpit (G7, G8, G9) | $400-$600 |
| Pinch vase (G10) | $500-$600 |
| Bud vase (G11) | $300-$500 |
| Shoulder vase (G12) | $100-$500 |

Compotes

| | |
|---|---|
| Ruffled top (G13) | $250-$350 |
| Smooth rim (G14) | $200-$350 |
| Hollow stem (G15) | $350-$450 |
| Swirl connector (G16) | $500-$750 |

Console bowl (G17) — $250-$300

Paul Revere bowl (G18) — $300-$350

Cruets (G19, front, G20) — $900-$1,000

Handled decanters (G19, back) — $1,000-$1,200

Decanter, no handle (G21) — $1,000-$1,200

Perfume (G22) — $1,000-$1,200

Perfume, flowered stopper (G23) — no price

Perfume, paperweight flower stopper (G24) — $3,000-$5,000

Creamers

| | |
|---|---|
| Bulbous (G25) | $200-$300 |
| Ribbed (G26) | $250-$300 |
| Same as above, not ribbed | $225-$275 |
| One long handle (G26) | $300-$350 |

Sugars

| | |
|---|---|
| Ribbed (G27) | $250-$300 |
| Not ribbed, no handles (G28) | $200-$300 |

Milk pitcher (G29) — $300-$500

Bulbous pitcher (G30) — $250-$350

Sherbet (G31) — $250-$350

Goblets/chalices, Burmese feet (G32) — $250-$300 ea.

Wine (G33) — $100-$150

Candlesticks, crimped top (G34) — $500-$750 pair

Candlesticks, waterfall (G35) — $200-$300 pair

Basket (G36) — no price

Paperweight (G37) — no price

Luncheon plate (G38) — $200-$300

Swan (G39) — no price

Cup and saucer (G40) — $150-$250

## Chapter 8: Pairpoint Peachblow

Swan (P1) — $35-$50

Tiny duck (P2) — $50-$75

Bell (P3) — $350-$500

Tiny pitcher (P4) — $25-$50

Large vase (P5) — $150-$250

Millefiore vase (P6) — $100-$150

Lily vase (P7) — $150-$200

Trumpet vases (P8) — $150-$200 ea.

Hats (P9)

| | |
|---|---|
| Decorated | $125-$225 |
| Undecorated | $50-$100 |

| | |
|---|---|
| Ruffled vases (P11, P13) | $50-$75 |
| Jack-in-the-pulpit, C. Bryden decoration (P15) | $250-$350 |
| Jack-in-the-pulpit, metal base (P16) | $100-$150 |
| Plate/shallow bowl (P17) | $75-$125 |
| Basket (P18) | $150-$250 |
| Small plate or saucer (P20) | $100-$150 |
| Candlestick (P21) | $75-$125 |
| Compote Kiluk decoration (P22) | $250-$300 |
| Compote (P23) | $150-$200 |
| Compote, ruffled foot and top (P24) | no price |
| Goblet (P25) | $150-$250 |
| Flower form (P25) | $100-$200 |
| Compote (P25) | $100-$175 |
| Small ruffled vase (P26) | $100-$150 |
| Sugar bowls (P27) | $100-$150 |
| Creamer, heart shape (P28) | $100-$150 |
| Creamer, bulbous (P29) | $75-$125 |
| Creamer and sugar, ribbed (P30) | $75-$150 set |
| Vases (P32) | $75-$150 ea. |
| Various items (P33) | $75-$150 |
| Various items (P34) | $75-$200 |

## Chapter 9: Italian Peachblow

| | |
|---|---|
| Italian "Mt. Washington" peachblow | $60-$100 ea. |
| Italian "Wheeling peachblow" | no available data |
| Italian cranberry to blue "peachblow" | no available data |

## Chapter 10: Bennett Peachblow

| | |
|---|---|
| Smaller shapes | $55-$75 |
| Larger shapes | $125-$175 |

## Chapter 11: Fenton Peach Blow

| | |
|---|---|
| 1939 line | no available data |
| 1939 line | $35-$75 ea. |
| Hobnail, small items | $45-$70 ea. |
| (More for basket, hurricane lamp) | |

## Chapter 12: L. G. Wright Peach Blow

| | |
|---|---|
| Rose bowls, undecorated, pink shaded over white (LGW4, LGW5) | $60-$85 |
| Rose bowls, moss rose decoration (LGW6) | $65-$95 |
| Rose bowls, white over pink, no decoration (LGW8) | $30-$45 |
| Rose bowls, embossed rose pattern (LGW23) | $40-$65 |
| Rose bowl, maize (LGW9) | $85-$110 |
| Rose bowl, beaded curtain (LGW10) | $95-$110 |
| Lamps, moss rose, all sizes | $250-$500 |
| Lamps, embossed rose | $250-$500 |
| Lamp, beaded curtain, all sizes (LGW20) | $300-$500 |
| Vase, moss rose | $90-$100 |
| Creamer, moss rose | $85-$125 |
| Cruet, moss rose | $95-$125 |
| Tumbler, moss rose (undecorated, less) | $55-$65 |
| Pitcher, moss rose | $250-$300 |
| Fairy lamp, decorated | $250-$400 |

## Chapter 13: Imperial Peachblow

| | |
|---|---|
| Vases | $125-$175 |
| Decanters | $275-$300 |

## Chapter 14: Pilgrim Peachblow

| | |
|---|---|
| Miniature items | $10-$15 |
| Larger decanters | $25-$35 |

## Chapter 15: Kanawha Peachblow

| | |
|---|---|
| Small items | $15-$20 |
| Larger items | $25-$35 |

## Chapter 16: Intaglio Peachblow

| | |
|---|---|
| Rose bowls | $25-$35 |
| Other items | no available data |

# Index